The Ultimate Guide to Newsletters: Your Secret Weapon for Doubling Referrals and Tripling Retention

www.TheNewsletterPro.com

ISBN: 978-1539142850

Printed in the United States of America

Second Edition

Previously published as *Newsletter Marketing: Insider Secrets to Using Newsletters to Increase Profits, Get More New Customers, and Keep Customers Longer Than You Ever Thought Possible.* (Copyright © 2013 Shaun Buck)

Design and layout by The Newsletter Pro.

THE ULTIMATE GUIDE TO NEWSLETTERS:
Your Secret Weapon for Doubling Referrals and Tripling Retention

NEED HELP WITH YOUR NEWSLETTER? TALK TO THE PROS.

Schedule a complimentary consultation with our team by visiting www.thenewsletterpro.com/schedule.

REVIEWS FROM AMAZON

Check out the reviews on this book's first edition— *Newsletter Marketing: Insider Secrets to Using Newsletters to Increase Profits, Get More New Customers, and Keep Customers Longer Than You Ever Thought Possible*

One of the Best Newsletter Books, Plus It's a Detailed Marketing Primer

"Shaun Buck's book goes far beyond just newsletters. So much so, that you could throw away any number of your marketing books and just do what he tells you in this little book. This book also lays out the essentials that ANY successful business needs to have, in order to market effectively." – Walter

Read Only If You Want Your Business to Grow

"If you are a small-business owner, this is a must-read. Shaun's information will enable you to put yourself in front of your customers time and time again. Something we small-business owners lack. I highly recommend this read for anyone looking to grow their business. [Shaun's] insight and knowledge is unparalleled; clearly newsletters are the way to go." – Al

Building Relationships That Matter. Personal. Professional. Powerful.

A Must-Read for Small-Business Owners

"This book is filled with great actionable plans to get your newsletter going from start to finish. Plenty of great examples as well as numerous reasons why starting a newsletter is in your best interest. It's a quick and easy read that will provide great value for your business." – David

Excellent Book

"Shaun is the dean of newsletters. He has a unique way of connecting with the reader and is able to provide a ton of actionable content. This is a great book for anyone who wants to learn how to use a newsletter to take their business to the next level. I would recommend that all business owners, small and large, take the time to read this book." – Adam

Newsletters Are Critical

"A newsletter keeps us in front of our customers and potential customers. What Shaun has outlined in this book—and given in reprints of some articles—is pure content that gives us an idea of what to do in our newsletters. If you are hesitating, don't. Call Shaun and discuss your questions and hesitations—he is a master at this stuff. And he gets results. Five stars? I wish there were six." – Robert

The REAL Truth About This Book!

"I got Buck's book and had a four-page, full-color newsletter mailed to my top 500 list within 30 days of reading it... If you want to finally get your newsletter done, read the dang book, or skip the book and go 20 years thinking about having a newsletter. Just be sure to pray each evening that none of your competitors read Buck's book!" – Wally

Killer Ideas in This One!

"I loved not only the super fun and conversational writing style of the author, but the ideas included were fantastic too! My understanding of newsletters—the ins and outs, whys and why nots—has grown substantially! I would definitely recommend this book to any small-business owner who is looking for an awesome how-to for newsletter marketing!" – Mandi

Informative and Entertaining

"The information in this book is invaluable, and every business owner should read it, and then read it again. I have already started to implement some of the strategies I picked up—and I am starting to see my ROI take an upswing. I can't wait to see what the next few months of following Shaun's philosophies can do for my business!" – Gracie

DEDICATION

Thank you, Lord, for your mercy and blessings, which you give me on a daily basis.

To my beautiful wife, Mariah: Thank you for the love and support you've shown me over the years. I am so glad we are taking the rest of this journey through life together. Also, thank you for being such an awesome mom to our five boys. I love you.

To Brandon: It has been a crazy, fun, and exciting 20 years since you were born. I could never have imagined back then how great a young man you would become. I owe much of my success to having you in my life, and I want you to know that I love you very much and am proud of the man you have become.

To Tyler: If there were ever a born entrepreneur, it would be you. You are funny, handsome, smart, and charismatic. I enjoy watching you grow every day. Keep up the great job you are doing of being a big brother to all of your little brothers. They look up to you, and for good reason. Keep working hard, and don't worry about getting a no when you're out selling stuff to the neighbors. Those two skills alone will get you far in life.

To Jeremiah: Your smile and laugh can melt my heart. You are so sweet, kind, and lovey. You make me happy daily. I love watching you be a kid. From capturing bugs and frogs to making up games with your brothers, you get to enjoy being a kid, and that makes me so very happy, because you and your brothers getting to have an amazing childhood is my reason why.

To Alexander: You are such a sweet and handsome boy with your crazy, red hair and beautiful, green eyes. I love how special God made you. You are so very sweet and passionate. You give everything to all you want to do. You're naturally gifted in athletics of all kinds and have a bright future in whatever you choose to do in life. I know you have a hard time each and every day when I walk out the door, but know I work hard daily for you and your brothers, with a goal of giving you the best childhood possible.

To Kellen: Do you ever stop smiling? I love the way you laugh and simply enjoy life. You are sweet, kind, and simply amazing. I can't believe how big you're getting. It is so rare to see a kid as happy as you are all the time. Don't lose that as you get older. Keep on being sweet and caring. It will serve you well in life.

To my dad: Thank you for your support and friendship over the years. It may seem silly to some, but I hope I've made you proud. Also, for the record, I believe I have gone above and beyond the call of duty, when it comes to keeping the family name alive and strong. Five boys!

To my mom: Last of my thank-yous, but certainly not the least. Mom, I want you to know I love you, and just in case I haven't told you, I appreciate all you did for us kids growing up. You worked hard, and from my point of view, always did what you thought was in our best interest. I am not sure what more a kid could ask for. By the way, I know how much you enjoy reading, so I hope you enjoy this book—and I love you.

TABLE OF CONTENTS

CHAPTER 1

The Newsletter Pro

I have taken a different path than most to becoming an entrepreneur. I could go all the way back to being 10 or 11 years old and give the history of what drove me to want to be a business owner. But that isn't the purpose of this book and is possibly better left to someone with bigger titles and more college degrees than I have to fully analyze.

But before I jump into how you too can grow your business with newsletters, I do want to take a moment to introduce myself and give you a bit of my story because I think it is important for you to understand a little about me, my entrepreneurial philosophy, and how I ended up publishing and mailing millions of newsletters each year.

It all started when I was just a wee baby. Nah, I'm just kidding. I told you we'd skip that.

In 1995, at age 16, I got a phone call that would change my life forever. It was my ex-girlfriend, and she was calling to tell me she was pregnant. At first, I was confused. We had been broken up for about two months, and I wondered to myself why she was calling *me* to share the news. My confusion ended quickly when she uttered those four magic words: "The baby is yours." I thought she was joking and even told her I didn't think that was very funny, but I quickly realized (when she stared crying) that it wasn't a joke at all.

Of course, I had the standard questions any 16-year-old boy would have, like "Are you sure?" and "How did this happen?" Some of the questions (of course) were rhetorical, as I knew how babies were made, but like most kids at 16, I wasn't really thinking about the future and what could happen. To be fair to 16-year-olds, some people I know now at 37 don't think about what may happen in the future, so I guess it isn't just a teenage thing.

A few short months after that call, I was faced with the dilemma of how I was going to help take care of a baby, go to school, and maybe even try to work things out with my baby's mama. I have always been a pretty smart guy, so it didn't take me long to realize that my job at Chuck E. Cheese's—playing the mouse on weekends and bussing tables on weekdays, and making a whopping $4.50 per hour—was not going to be much help.

So I did what anyone would do. I quickly dropped out of high school and got a "real job" selling some fancy, modern home computers with this new thing called a Pentium®

processor to power them. Doesn't it just make you feel old thinking back to 1995? Sure does for me as I type this.

Good news—at the new job, I not only got health insurance after 90 days, but in my first month, I made $4,800. I also won a trip to Vegas and some prize money, for selling a ton of Apple computers—and that was before Apple was cool, I might add. Unfortunately, I had to be 21 to claim the trip and prize money.

I did ultimately go back to school via distance learning and charter schools, and I got my diploma. Woo-hoo! My baby was born—a healthy, beautiful baby boy, whom we named Brandon. As I write this, Brandon is 20 years old and one of the most AWESOME people I have ever had the pleasure of knowing.

Things didn't work out with me and my baby's mama, but in 1999, I met the love of my life. We married and since have had four more boys.

Let me hit pause here because I know what you're thinking—*five boys?* Yes, five boys. On a side note, I have been trying to convince Mariah, my wife, that it is obvious I only make boys, so with just a little planning, we could toss this whole entrepreneur thing out and get our own TV show called *Shaun and Mariah, Plus Eight Boys*. Doesn't that have a nice ring to it?

Alright let me un-pause and get back to our story. As far as education goes, I went to Solano Community College for a bit, where I took business classes along with general education. I did not graduate from college with a degree. During my college experience was when I started what I call my first "real" business. The reason I call it real is because it was more than just cutting lawns for a few people in the neighborhood or selling pagers to the kids at school. But more on that in a minute.

The reason I left college is actually kind of humorous. After class one day, I was talking to the primary business professor at the school, when he told me that he had never *owned* a business before. *What?* And here I was taking a class from him on business *when I had more real-life business experience than he did!* As you can imagine, that was the end of that. I finished the semester and never went back.

Let me slow down a little on the first real business part, as this is a business book. At the ripe old age of 21, I bought a Woody's Hot Dogs franchise for $45,000, which gave me the hot dog stand itself and the right to open it in front of a brand-new Lowe's Home Improvement store. I know what you're thinking—45,000 bucks is a ton of cash for a 21-year-old—but I had some money saved up and had great credit, plus, in 2001, money flowed uphill, so there you go.

I won't spend a ton of time on this topic, but for some reason, people like this story, so here it is: We opened the stand in August 2001 and sold over $20,000 in hot dogs and sodas that month alone. Over the coming months, we did so well that we bought another Woody's Hot Dogs stand in front of another new Lowe's Home Improvement store, about 30 minutes from our first location. Between the two stands, we sold $400,000 to $450,000 a year in hot dogs. That's a lot of hot dogs.

So the name is Woody's Hot Dogs, and the slogan is, "It's the big one baby, it's a Woody." That still cracks me up every time.

Alright, back to the story. Even with great sales, I quickly realized that there were some major flaws in our business model. For example, even though I was in California, it was cold in the winter standing outside for eight-plus hours a day. The margins were slim because people were stealing from us, and on and on and on.

With all the problems and the discovery that I didn't actually *like* the hot dog stand business, I started looking for a new franchise to buy and people to sell the hot dog stands to. Looking for a new franchise is what led me to discovering newsletters.

Hear Shaun talk more about his story on the Gold Call interview with Dave Dee on "The Most Powerful Tool in Your Marketing Arsenal." If you haven't heard it yet, you can download the MP3 file at www.thenewsletterpro.com/book-resources.

CHAPTER 2

My First Introduction to Newsletters

Once I had decided it was time to start or buy another business, I did what any young entrepreneur would do: I started requesting things like uniform franchise offering circulars and franchise agreements from a few dozen franchisers. For many, that stuff would have put them to sleep, but I enjoyed reading about these businesses, how they made money, and even all the legal mumbo jumbo. Even as a kid, I loved business and numbers. That enjoyment only grew as I got older. I know; I'm weird.

Along with the franchise agreements, I got all kinds of sales materials and sales phone calls, but after a month or two, the sales calls had all but stopped. I don't know about other people who buy franchises, but I wasn't going to be rushed into a decision. Out of the few dozen franchises I had looked into, only one franchiser—a dry cleaning business—kept in contact with me on a regular basis, mainly via an eight- to 16-page monthly newsletter, and I loved that newsletter. It had many of the aspects that make up a GREAT newsletter. Here are a few examples:

- Personal article from the founder of the company

- Top 10 list of franchises

- New franchise interview

- Success stories from existing franchises

- Business-building ideas and tips

- Promotion for the upcoming franchise convention

- Updates on new products and services the franchiser would be rolling out

It really was a very well-done newsletter. On a side note, it was so well-done that to this day, I still have every copy.

Every time one of these newsletters came in the mail, I opened it and devoured the contents. I read it cover to cover, and then gave it to my girlfriend (now my lovely wife) to read so we could talk about it. I thoroughly enjoyed getting that newsletter each month and hearing about the success others were having and seeing the top 10 lists. I even felt as though I had a personal relationship with the CEO, who happened to be one of the people who was trying to get me to part with my $20,000 and sign a 10-year contract to do business with her company. My girlfriend and

I would spend hours talking about what we read, about what it would be like to own that kind of a business, and about the franchise itself.

This company's newsletter was doing nearly everything right. In fact, the company was doing such a good job that I did end up buying their franchise, sooner than I had wanted to.

Want to take a guess as to why I bought earlier than I had planned? I wanted to become part of the company so I could attend the annual convention. I was very excited about everything they were going to teach at the convention and felt that I would be missing out if I didn't buy early and attend. Considering the relationship I felt I had with the CEO, the excitement I felt, and the growth I was reading about in the newsletter involving new and existing franchise owners, I couldn't help myself. That newsletter was the hook.

When I was looking to buy a franchise, I considered companies that were large and small. I was interested in a few of them, but not a single franchiser, other than the dry cleaning franchise I ended up buying, stayed in contact with me. None of

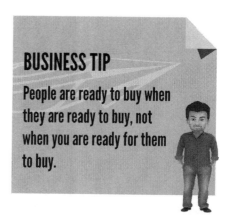

BUSINESS TIP

People are ready to buy when they are ready to buy, not when you are ready for them to buy.

them followed up for longer than two months after I first contacted them. And ultimately, all of them missed out not only on the initial franchise fee, but also on the ongoing franchise fees I paid.

Because people are ready to buy when they are ready to buy, you MUST communicate with them on a regular and consistent basis. Studies have shown that 18 percent of people are impulse buyers; 82 percent of people take three months to make a buying decision; and a whopping 61 percent of people take greater than 12 months to make a buying decision.

When someone inquirers about your product or service and, within weeks, you stop communicating with them, how many of those prospects that aren't ready to buy now turn into good, using customers? How much money are you leaving on the table, when, six months or 12 months from now, that prospect is finally ready to buy? Unless you communicate on a regular basis using a media they will pay attention to, your prospect, whom you spent money on to get to call in, now raises their hand and identifies as a potential new customer, but has no clue who you are, what you do, or even that you are still in business.

Just the other day, I had a lawyer call who was looking to get started with newsletters for his practice. When my team pulled his info up in our customer relationship management software (CRM) they found I had last spoken with him 18 months earlier. This lawyer and his firm were now ready to become customers of ours and ended up enrolling in our program to mail over 3,000 newsletter per month, which is a good sized customer. It's likely he wouldn't have signed up with us if he hadn't been receiving regular communication from us via our monthly newsletter.

If someone's not buying today, that doesn't mean they won't be interested in buying from you tomorrow. You never know why someone didn't buy right away, but it's your job as the business owner to make sure your company is nurturing prospects and guiding them to making a buying decision.

CHAPTER 3
My First Newsletter

As you can imagine, since newsletters did so well in helping the dry cleaning franchiser sell franchises, they had a section of their contract that required you to write and publish your own two- to four-page newsletter. That was very smart of the franchiser, but what was dumb (I mean *really* dumb) was that they left the writing and publishing up to us franchisees.

At the time, I wasn't a writer. Heck, I was glad to have made it through English in college. I didn't know the first thing about putting together a newsletter, and the franchiser had exactly zero training for us franchisees.

Building Relationships That Matter. Personal. Professional. Powerful.

My first edition was a train wreck! To be fair, almost all of my editions were train wrecks. To make sure you fully appreciate just how bad they were, let me share with you an example of one of my first newsletters.

** See example on next page

WELCOME!

We would like to welcome all of our customers to the DRY CLEANING TO-YOUR-DOOR→☐ (DCTYD) family.

You are joining tens of thousands of other customers around the country. We appreciate your business!

Deodorant Residue

Prolonged contact with deodorants may cause permanent damage. Combined with perspiration overuse of these products or infrequent cleaning causes buildup of residue or fabric damage. Antiperspirants contain aluminum chloride, which may change the color of some dyes. Residue buildup and chemical damage can occur resulting in a permanent color change of the fabric. To prevent damage, do not overuse the product and allow it to dry before dressing. Wear dress shields with silk garments.

Information From: Clothes Care Gazette. No. 175

The Secret to Removing Grass Stains

Most grass stains can be removed by simply washing the item according to the care instructions, especially if the stain is fresh. But if the stain has been allowed to set or proves to be difficult to remove you may need to try other treatments.

Treat the stain as soon as possible, using a pretreatment product from your local store. Test the product for colorfastness by applying it to an unexposed area. Let the garment stand for five minutes, then rinse. If the color is affected don't use the product. Also, check the label on your laundry detergent for pretreatment instructions. To remove any last traces try an all-fabric bleach. Again, remember to test for colorfastness. Bleach the entire garment following the manufacturer's instructions, then launder as usual. Of course, if you still need help getting the stain out, let your professional dry cleaner have a crack at it – THAT'S US! Just make a note pointing out the stain and what you've already used on the garment. We have tons of experience with these types of stains!

Where Did That Stain Come From?

"But it wasn't there before!"

Have you ever looked at a garment after cleaning and noticed spots or stains that simply weren't there when you brought it in?

We call these "invisible stains," and beverages most often cause them.

Here's what happens. Let's say you spill soda or some other beverage on your shirt and it dries clear. However upon exposure to heat, most stains will turn yellow or brown. This change in color is caused by oxidation of sugar found in most beverages. Unfortunately, this problem isn't just limited to sodas: Any beverage with sugar or alcohol can cause this staining problem.

If you are not familiar with the oxidation process. Here's a simple way to understand it. Think about what happens to an apple when you peel it and leave it out for a brief time. It turns brown. This is an example of oxidation!

Another type of "invisible stain" occurs when an oily substance is exposed to heat or ages in a garment for an extended time. This type of stain can be recognized by an irregular cross pattern that the oil makes. Once oily substances are left to oxidize, they can become yellow or brown and are extremely difficult to remove.

Here's what you can do to help us out: Point out any stains to us, so we can treat them before subjecting the garment to heat from drying or pressing. Mark the areas with a piece of tape so we know where the stain is. Otherwise, the stain may go undetected through the cleaning process and could become permanently set in the fabric. We have the knowledge and expertise required to handle "invisible stains." If we can get to them before they are exposed to heat, we can return your garment to you in excellent condition! So don't be afraid to tell us where and when those stains occurred!

WE APPRECIATE YOUR BUSINESS!

Shaun Buck * P.O. Box 6687 Vacaville, CA 95696 * 707-422-6100 * September 2002
"America's Finest FREE Home Pick-Up, NEXT DAY Delivery Dry Cleaning Service"

Honestly, the fact that I ever published that newsletter is embarrassing. Do people in their right minds really want to read about deodorant residue or invisible stains? If I could nominate this newsletter for the award of "Most Boring," I would. I have even heard rumors that a few people keep this book by their nightstand, and if they ever have a case of insomnia, they simply open the book and read my very first newsletter. Like magic, within minutes, they're sleeping like babies.

BUSINESS TIP

Even if it's a great idea, an idea that is poorly executed or NOT executed at all won't get you the results you're looking for.

BUSINESS TIP

The biggest sin in marketing (for all kinds of marketing) is to be boring. If your marketing and newsletter are currently boring, I have two words for you—stop it!

I mailed this newsletter for two whole years before I eventually figured out that people will not read boring articles. And if they are not going to read boring articles, they surely are not going to read a whole boring newsletter.

I see others making this mistake all the time. The biggest sinners, when it comes to boring newsletters, are dentists. Does anyone want to read a newsletter filled with stories about drilling teeth, gum disease, and tooth decay? Of course not. It is estimated that 76 percent of the population has some kind of fear of dentists, so in this particular case, I guarantee no one is reading those newsletters.

If you are sitting there thinking, *"But my business is different,"* let me assure you it is not. Boring is boring. If you publish boring, no matter what business or industry you are in, no one is going to read it. Think of this: Who makes more money—entertainers or teachers? Of course entertainers do. We live in a time in history where people are consumed with being entertained all day, every day. With distractions like the internet, 250 TV channels, cell phones, millions of songs, and a whole library of books on everyone's iPads, no one is going to pay one once of attention to you if you are giving them boring content.

CHAPTER 4

8 Ways Newsletters Will Grow Your Sales and Profits

As business owners, we're always looking to grow our bottom line. With that in mind, I've put together eight ways that a newsletter can drastically grow your sales and add profits. At The Newsletter Pro, we know that newsletters have an impact on these areas because we see the results. Plus, we have customers who've told us the same thing and who are currently experiencing a growth of sales and profits in their own businesses.

No. 1 – Newsletters Increase Customer Lifetime Value (LTV)

Every month you don't communicate with your customers, the relationship value you've built will decrease. It is estimated that on average, you lose 10 percent or more of your overall goodwill and relationship value with the customer, each month he doesn't hear from you. It is also estimated that after six months of not communicating with your customer, your advantage is lost, and you're nearly on the same playing field as any one of your competitors. At that point, your customer can be stolen away easily, even if your competitors are only presenting a mildly intriguing coupon, discount, or offer. I don't know about you, but that sounds like bad news to me.

The single toughest challenge for ANY business is to acquire new customers. If you're letting these new customers get taken over to the dark side—and by dark side, I mean to any of your competitors—frankly, that pretty much sucks. Worse, if on the last time that customer did business with you, they had a problem, or their overall customer experience was below-average, the speed at which the customer can become disenchanted with your business is accelerated. And guess what? It actually gets worse than that.

The issue that caused the customers to feel upset may not even be an issue they shared with you. Even if they did bring the problem to your attention, it is entirely possible that they shared it with you but told you it wasn't a big deal. So you brushed it off, only for them to receive a competitor's offer in the mail a few weeks later, and afterward, never use you again. This scenario, or something close to it, happens thousands of times every day. You can no longer afford to take customers for granted.

The sheer volume of choice every consumer has nowadays requires you to sit up and pay attention. I'm sure you know who your competitors are, but many people don't realize how small of a pond they are playing in. Have you ever heard someone comment about the vast numbers of Starbucks in America? They seem to be everywhere, right? Here is an interesting fact: Did you know that there are 14 dental offices in America for every Starbucks? Likewise, there are over 1.22 million lawyers in the U.S. The number of new lawyers in the U.S. has tripled in the last 35 years, though the overall population has only risen 40 percent in the same time frame. Not to mention, there's the competition coming from the internet, providing sites like LegalZoom.com and others. Competition has increased for everyone, which is why it is becoming increasingly more difficult and costly to acquire a new customer.

That increase in cost for customer acquisitions requires that entrepreneurs be less sloppy with how they conduct business. The top 1 percent of any industry has a way to protect their customers from the competition, and the single best way to do that is by building a relationship. People prefer to do business with people they know and like; you just have to find a way to build that relationship on a mass scale.

Losing customers is a natural occurrence for any business. The problem is that many business owners either have no clue what their customer cancellation rate is, or they chalk up their retention issues to being "normal" for their industry. Some level of client loss is normal because people do move and do die, and frankly, you can't please everyone 100 percent of the time. But most businesses don't have any clue they have a retention problem, let alone how to fix it, because they have never bothered to check what their attrition rate is.

A lack of communication is a major factor in low customer retention. According to a study done by the Rockefeller

Corporation, 68 percent of people stop doing business with a company because they perceive indifference. Why would a customer think a business was indifferent to them? After all, businesses need customers; it's how they pay the bills and make money, right?

If you look at the way most businesses treat their customers, you begin to understand why so many customers feel that the companies they do business with are indifferent to them. At The Newsletter Pro, we always say you don't want to be "that guy." What we're referring to is "that guy" we all know—the one who only calls to hit you up for a favor or money. Think about how most businesses treat their customers. Most businesses only call or write when they want something. They may want a bill paid or to sell you more stuff, but that is the only time they communicate. When you are faced with a "that guy" scenario in your personal life, how does it make you feel? Do you dread getting that call? Do you feel annoyed, thinking to yourself, *"Not again..."*? The answer is probably yes. So why do business owners think that when they treat customers in the same manner, the customer feels any differently about them? Don't be that guy.

By publishing a monthly newsletter, you'll be able to reach out to your customers once a month, drastically increasing the amount of communication you have with them. And when you create a newsletter your customers enjoy reading (which I will explain how to do later in the book), you will see an increase in their lifetime value (LTV). The LTV of customers is a very important number for your business. Let's take a look at some basic business math and explore this concept further.

Some of the Most Important Math You Can Do to Understand and Grow Your Business

If the average customer in your business has a gross profit for your company of $175 per month, and that same average customer typically does business with you for eight months, that makes your average customer LTV $1,400 in gross profit. Now, let me ask you a question: How much would you happily spend to get more of these new customers? Okay, so we need more info about the business to come up with the *exact* right answer of how much we would spend, but for the purpose of this hypothetical exercise, let's assume that you would be willing to spend two months' profits or $350 to get a new customer and keep them for eight months. You would turn a $1,050 profit, which would make your $350 investment a wise decision.

Alright, now let me take this a step further. Assume that you put in a customer retention campaign that increases the length of time your average customer stays with you by five months, so instead of keeping a customer for only eight months, you now keep them for 13. Also assume that your average gross profit per customer stays at $175 per month, bringing your total gross profit per average customer to $2,275. Now, how much would you be willing to spend to get another customer? In our imaginary scenario, spending

$700 or four months of profits would be completely reasonable to get a good average customer. After spending your $700, you'd still have a profit of $1,575, which is $525 greater than your original profit per customer, despite the fact that you are spending up to 200 percent more to acquire each new customer.

If you were able spend double the amount of money to acquire a new customer, do you think you would be able find additional ways of getting new customers? Of course you would. Just for fun, let me ask you this: Do you think your ability to spend money on advertising that your competitors can't afford is going to piss them off? Of course it is. Confused and upset competition is always a good thing.

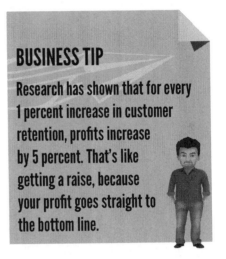

BUSINESS TIP

Research has shown that for every 1 percent increase in customer retention, profits increase by 5 percent. That's like getting a raise, because your profit goes straight to the bottom line.

Most people are missing out on a massive opportunity to increase the LTV of their average customer. All they have to do is keep in touch with their customers on a regular basis. I don't want you to miss this opportunity; it is so important to your overall business success.

Our example scenario doesn't take into account these important facts:

- Typically, the longer customers are with you, the better customers they become (i.e., they spend more, more often, and are easier to sell additional products and services to). I will go into more detail later in the book on this subject.

- With five extra months of using your company, each customer now has five more months to refer new business to you.

- The most successful businesses always figure out how they can spend the most to acquire each new customer, where average businesses are always looking to figure out how to spend the least on acquiring each new customer.

No. 2 – Newsletter Help You Stay Top of Mind

We live in a world that is SO busy. Most of us can't even remember what we were doing at 2:15 p.m. three days ago, let alone the name of the new dentist we went to or the law firm that won us a bunch of money six months ago. But that is not what most business owners think. Most business owners think that once a person has done business with them, that customer now knows who they are, and everything the business sells (more on the "everything you sell" thought process later). I hate to be the bearer of bad news, but nothing could be further from the truth.

Have you ever met someone at a party or social gathering, or even at church, and had

BUSINESS TIP

"My single biggest recommendation is the use of a monthly customer newsletter. Nothing, and I mean nothing, maintains your fence [around your customers] better."

– Dan Kennedy

a very nice conversation with them for 10 or 20 minutes, only to have no clue what that person's name is two hours later, when you're telling the story to your wife? I've actually had conversations with the same people from church every week for months and, even now, still struggle with their names. You may think that makes me a not-so-nice person, but I'm not doing it to be mean. The truth of the matter is, it happens to most of us. One of the reasons I still might not know someone's name after months of talking to them is simple embarrassment. I feel bad that I don't know their name, and I can't ask them a second time.

It's illogical to assume that just because someone does business with you a few times, they're going to know who you are weeks or months later. But that's how business owners act. When you hire a new employee, you know it can take months for them to memorize all the products and services you offer, but new customers are supposed to know in three visits?

A study done a few years ago by Yankelovich, a market research firm, found that a person living in the city 30 years ago likely saw up to 2,000 ad messages a day, compared to upward of 5,000 today. I would be willing to bet that in the last decade, give or take, since that study was done, the number of ads we see on any given day has increased drastically. Now we have ads on our cell phones, in our text messages, on all the social media sites, in our email, on the TV, on the radio as we drive to work, in the magazines we read, and on and on and on.

With at least as many as two-and-a-half times more advertising messages being delivered to us as the number of ads our parents received, it is no wonder we can't remember the name of the law firm that settled our case 27 days ago or the name of our finical planner's company. To make matters worse, some businesses just have names that are hard to remember and even harder to spell.

The fact that we can't remember is part one of a HUGE problem we business owners face. The second part of the problem is if your new and existing customers can't remember the name of your business, how in the world are they ever going to refer new business to you? The answer: They won't. Even worse than not getting a referral, if they can't remember your name, how are they going to do ANY business with you again? If you are thinking people aren't forgetting who you are, where you are, and what you do, think again. These two reasons are enough to support sending a monthly print newsletter.

One area of business that is struggling greatly with this is the professional practice sector—doctors, dentists, and lawyers. In years past, it was nearly enough to simply hang out your shingle and watch business pour in, but now that is not the case. Of course, there are many reasons for this, such as increased competition, for example. But a huge factor is the lack of referrals from existing patients or clients, and this is a problem that is affecting all markets. Another HUGE problem facing all business owners is increased competition. You can easily see that a 150 percent increase in the number of advertising messages being delivered, in and of itself, shows a massive increase in competition, which makes it more important than ever to stay top of mind with your customers. If they can't remember your name, it is nearly impossible for them to do business with you again or give you a referral.

By sending a monthly customer newsletter, you drastically increase the ability for your customers and even prospects to remember your name when it is time for them to do business with you again or give you a referral of a friend or family member.

No. 3 – It Is Easier to Increase Sales With Existing Customers Than It Is to Find New Customers

As I talked about in point No. 2, by sending a monthly newsletter, you get the benefit of people being able to remember your name and, in turn, being more likely to do business with you again. In this section, I want to go over how to get those returning customers to spend more money with you.

Once you have conquered one of the hardest aspects of business, which is getting a person to open up their wallet and spend real money with you, you have the start of a relationship with your new customer. If you can prove to them that you have a good product or service and that you provide good customer service, you'll also be given a degree of trust. Furthermore, you'll have a degree of familiarity, which makes the second sale to the same customer infinitely easier than the first sale. That familiarity and level of trust also increases your new, satisfied customer's willingness to spend more with you, even on higher-priced products and services.

Here is the rub, though—most business owners overlook or abuse the relationship and/or the trust that has been placed in them. It is this indifference to or abuse of the relationship that causes most business owners to lose the goodwill they have established. That makes the second sale to these customers almost as difficult as the first sale. The indifference/abuse also has a side effect, whereby these customers you have worked so hard to get become very easy for your competitors to poach.

It is very important that, as business owners, you don't have an indifference to the relationship you have with your customers/prospects. Obviously, what you really want is to grow that relationship so you have the opportunity to both service them again and sell them additional products and services in the future.

That still begs the question, how do you use a newsletter to sell them more products or services? There are several ways to do this, but let's focus on three primary strategies.

1. Use Free-Standing Inserts (FSIs)

Being the "newsletter pro," I get to see a ton of newsletters, and one of the most common mistakes I see people making is putting blatant ads directly inside their newsletters. So there is no misunderstanding, it's not that I have a problem with the ads, but you don't want people to be reading your newsletter with their advertising shields up. Once you start putting ads in your newsletter, some people's perceptions of the newsletter change from it being a publication to it being an advertisement (i.e., junk mail), and that is the LAST thing you want. So the best way to put ads in your newsletter is to use what is called a free-standing insert, or FSI for short.

The FSI is a separate piece of paper either stuffed into the envelope or placed into the middle of a self-mailing newsletter. We have found this insert doesn't break the sanctity of the newsletter publication itself and is the best way to put a blatant ad in your newsletter.

At The Newsletter Pro, we use FSIs every month. Sometimes the FSI is for a straight offer (e.g., sign up today and get this cool widget for free). Many times we use the FSI as a lead generation piece where we try to reengage the reader by offering a lead magnet they can get for free. Since the people who end up pursuing that lead magnet are likely interested in the topic they got the lead magnet on, we follow up with them using a variety of offline and online media.

One other advanced technique we use for FSIs is segmenting our list. That means everyone on the list may get an FSI, but current customers get one FSI and prospects get a different FSI. This allows us to make offers more targeted to the reader.

Of course, there are exceptions to every rule, and I want to share a story with you of one exception for one of our clients that has worked out well.

We have a client who owns a large number of retail pet store chains. On the surface, many people would say that a newsletter wouldn't work for a retail pet store, but those people would be wrong. What we did was create an eight-page newsletter for this client. His newsletter has three pages of ads—the same type of ads you would normally see in the Sunday paper from a home goods store or clothing company. We print these ads directly into the newsletter and mail them to the company's top few thousand customers from each store, each month. They are able to track their customers' purchases via rewards cards, and they have found that not only are those top customers spending more in the stores per month, but they are also buying more of the advertised products.

For this client, an FSI is simply not necessary, as his products are the core of any retail business, and we have had great success with printing the ads in the newsletter in this instance. Sometimes rules are meant to be broken, but the average business is going to want to utilize FSIs instead of an ad printed directly into the newsletter.

2. Introduce New Products or Services

One of my favorite ways to increase sales is to present a new product or service in the newsletter. Of course, you have to be careful that this doesn't come off as too much of a sales pitch or look like an ad. My preferred method of presenting these new products or services is via a story. You can use pretty much any story, but my favorite story to use for this type of article is one that talks about how you found, developed, or stumbled upon this new product or service. The story works really well if you can also add some personal elements into it. That way, the story comes off more on the relationship and entertainment side instead of a straight pitch.

I have received some kickback on this idea from some of the more hardcore direct response marketing guys who prefer a straight pitch, but here is the thing: The primary purpose of a newsletter is to build relationships so you can get more referrals and increase your customer LTV. Don't destroy your readership to make a quick buck.

3. Promote Events

If you have an event of any kind coming up, using your newsletter and/or an FSI to promote that upcoming event is a great call. Make sure you plan post-event stories for the newsletter as well, so you can show how fun and successful the event was. By promoting the success of the event after it is completed, you end up with more attendance at future events.

BUSINESS TIP

If you want to improve these above strategies, consider following up your newsletter with a postcard and/or emails making the same offer. We've had great success turning our FSIs into multi-step campaigns that combine the FSI with a postcard and, when available, emails.

While we're on the topic of selling more to existing customers, I have found that many times business owners are so close to the daily operations of their businesses, they think, "Well, of course everyone knows what I do and what I sell." Unfortunately, that is not the case. I go back to the fact that people are busy, and even when it seems as though this information should be obvious, it's not.

I was reminded of this fact recently when I was attending a new mastermind group that I joined. I gave my introduction at the start of the day, telling everyone that my company creates fully custom newsletters for clients, as well as a few other details of the business. A few hours later, I was doing a more detailed presentation on my business when the person facilitating the group stopped me and said, "Shaun, let me make sure I understand you correctly. You create fully custom newsletters for companies, including interviewing the business owner and ghost writing the articles, plus the layout and editing?" I told them yes. The facilitator then asked whether anyone else had understood that about my business, and six or seven people said they hadn't realized that.

The fact that six or seven people (out of 10) hadn't realized that, in and of itself, wasn't surprising to me because I had only just met these people and given a 30-second introduction about my business. But when the facilitator, a guy whom I have gotten to know over the past year or so, said he didn't realize that we created fully customized newsletters for companies—that did surprise me. When I got back into the office, I checked my database and found out he wasn't on my monthly newsletter mailing list, which would explain how a guy I have known for a year or so was so taken aback by how we create newsletters for our clients. This experience taught me the importance of not only frequent communication, but of letting current clients know the extent of what you offer. They won't spend more with you if they don't know what their options are for additional products and services.

No. 4 – A Newsletter Will Build Your Expert/Celebrity Status.

A huge benefit of publishing a newsletter is that it builds your status as an expert and a celebrity. In our culture, we have been conditioned to think of people who get published as experts or celebrities. By publishing a monthly newsletter, you increase your expert status in the eyes of both your customers and your prospects.

Let me explain the difference between being an expert and being a celebrity.

Expert

As a culture, we like to do business with experts. We are happy to pay an expert more than the average Joe. We also are much more likely to take the advice of an expert.

Years ago, simply being a doctor, a dentist, or a lawyer would have been all you needed to be seen as an expert, but I can tell you for a fact, that is no longer true. I work with a number of these professionals, and I hear it all the time. A dentist can tell a patient that they need three fillings, but often patients need more evidence than the doctor's word to get those three fillings. Many people will simply wait until the tooth really hurts. Because of the loss of expert status, dentists have tons of patients who don't take the recommended treatments for one reason or another. This can cost a practice hundreds of thousands of dollars in lost production. If doctors, dentists, or lawyers— people who have gone through a massive amount of school to be given those titles and be seen in the eyes of the state as experts—are having a hard time being seen as experts, the road is much harder for us average folks.

One way to get that expert status is to be published and have your customers/prospects see the publication. The simplest way to get published is via your monthly newsletter. In the newsletter, you will have the opportunity to show you are an expert in your field above and beyond any degree you may have. To ensure all of your customers and prospects see it, all you have to do is pop a stamp on it. Plain and simple. Of course, you can't expect to be considered an expert from a single publication, but with ongoing publications, you will see an increase in people talking to you and treating you as an expert in your field.

Celebrity

We are a celebrity-obsessed culture. We reward celebrities with fame and riches. Some people even take it so far as to vote politically based on the opinions of a celebrity. As crazy as that truly is, it is the world we live in.

I want to ask you a hypothetical question. What would it do for your business if Oprah Winfrey, Donald Trump, or LeBron James endorsed your business? Obviously, your sales would skyrocket. That's why Nike and Wheaties and Coca-Cola all use celebrity endorsements.

That said, you likely do not have the marketing budget of Nike, Wheaties, or Coca-Cola, which may keep you from hiring one of those famous people, but you can always borrow celebrity or even turn yourself into a local celebrity. Whole books have been written on this topic. Since this is a book about newsletters, I'm not going to get into all the ins and outs of how to do this, but I will give you an overview.

Borrowing celebrity is as simple as getting your picture taken with a famous person and telling the story of how you met. For example, I recently met John Rich from the country band Big and Rich. John also won *The Celebrity Apprentice*, season 11. When I met John, I was in Tennessee, and after a short conversation, I asked him if he was going out on the town that night, and if so, could I join him? John has a huge reputation as a partier, and I can only imagine how cool it would be to party with a country music superstar.

With that conversation and a picture, I now have a story that can be used in my newsletter to build celebrity. Admittedly, the story would have been better if we'd partied, but unfortunately, after the event we were at, he was flying out to another event, so we didn't get to party like country music superstars. You can't win 'em all.

Now, that story may not resonate with everyone. Had John Rich not been on the *The Celebrity Apprentice*, I wouldn't have even known who he was, but it will slightly increase my celebrity with some people who do know who he is. That's because society believes you must be of some influence and importance to be meeting or hanging out with famous people.

For most businesses, simply becoming a local celebrity is good enough. To do this, you need to get published in local newspapers and magazines or be interviewed on radio or TV. In most cases, your appearance in the media will do little for your business, but by featuring the article or interview in your monthly newsletter, you increase your local celebrity.

No. 5 – Newsletters Build Relationships

As I mentioned in Chapter 1, I used to own a dry cleaning pickup and delivery business. Whenever I found someone who was using another cleaner in town, I would simply go and knock on their door and tell them about our service. Not the most fun or glamorous way to win new customers, but it worked.

There was one dry cleaning owner with whom I had a nearly 100 percent success rate at what he called "stealing" his customers. The reason my success rate with these customers was so high was because his prices were 50 to 100 percent greater than my prices or anyone else's in the market, and his quality and customer service didn't match his prices. But there was one exception to my near 100 percent ability to steal his customers.

Somehow, this guy had been able to build relationships—even friendships—with a larger than average number of his customers. I, of course, didn't know all of his tactics, but I did know he had some people over for dinner and went to sporting events with others. Because of those relationships, my success rate at stealing those particular customers dropped to about 10 percent. And likely, the only reason I was able to win over that small 10 percent was because of his crazy pricing. Of course, I showed the other 90 percent how I could nearly cut their dry cleaning bill in half, but I still could not get them to switch over to my service. That, my friend, is the power of a business relationship.

There are many ways to build a business relationship—one being to have one-on-one or one-on-many interactions with customers on a regular basis. One could argue that this is the best way to build not only a business relationship, but any relationship. That said, I don't know about you, but if I came to my wife and told her she had to help the business by having a customer's family over for dinner every Sunday night, she might make new permanent sleeping arrangements for me on the couch. So if you can't have all your customers over for dinner, what can you do? The next best way to build a business relationship is with your monthly newsletter.

Still not sold on the power of the business relationship? Let me relate a story that I heard from a mentor of mine, Dan Kennedy, that illustrates the power of a business relationship.

Imagine this—you are out doing yard work on a sunny afternoon when you cut your big toe open and start gushing blood all over the place. It's obvious you're going to need stitches. Since the cut is relatively minor, you decide not to make the 30-minute trek to your doctor's office and instead stop by the doc in the box office down the street. After the doctor you just met stitches up your big toe, he listens to your heart and checks a few other things. When he is done, he looks at you and says you have to get to the hospital immediately for open heart surgery or you may die. What do you do? If you are like most people, you quickly seek a second opinion. After all, you were simply there for stitches on your big toe.

Now, let's look at this same scenario, but let's make the doc in the box your longtime doctor whom you've been seeing for the past 20 years—the one you have a relationship with.

Again, you are on the table, but this time, it's your longtime doctor stitching you up. After she's finished, she listens to your heart and tells you that you need to get to the hospital right away for open heart surgery or you may die. You would likely ask her if she's sure. After all, you did just come in for stitches on your big toe. But then your doctor would say yes, she's sure, and so what would you do? Since you know this doctor and trust her, you're going to get your rear end to the hospital immediately.

That's the difference a relationship makes. But that leaves us with the question of how to build relationships with our customers. The easiest way is with a newsletter, and the easiest way to build those relationships with the newsletter is by adding a few personal stories each time. This will give people a peek behind the curtain into your life, as well as allow you to connect with them.

You might be thinking, *"No one cares what is going on in my life"* or *"My life is too boring and mundane to write an article a month about it."* I'm here to tell you that is not the case. Many people think the grass is greener on the other side, and they enjoy reading about other people's green grass. If you need proof, just look at *People* magazine or *Chicken Soup for the Soul*. Both of these publications spend a lot of time focusing on regular people and their stories, and both are massively popular. As of June 2014, here is a list, by circulation, of the top magazines in the U.S.

AARP the magazine – 22,837,736

AARP Bulletin – 22,183,316

Better Homes and Gardens – 7,639,661

Game Informer Magazine – 7,099,452

Good Housekeeping – 4,315,330

Family Circle – 4,015,728

National Geographic – 3,572,348

People – 3,510,533

Reader's Digest – 3,393,573

Woman's Day – 3,288,335

Eight out of 10 of the top 10 magazines are all about other people or helping people of a particular demographic have a better life. The odd ones out? *National Geographic* is about science and travel, and *Game Informer Magazine* is about video games. To be fair, playing video games is a hobby for some and could mean bettering their life. I guess it depends on your point of view, but either way, most of the top magazines in the U.S. include multiple stories about celebrities and/or regular people.

At the end of the day, people prefer to do business with people they know, like, and trust. It is your job to get people to know, like, and trust you. Short of inviting everyone over for dinner, it is hard to build those relationships on a large scale. But building relationships with your customers and prospects is one of the single most important things you can do for your business. People you have a relationship with will spend more money with you more frequently, will do business with you for longer periods of time, will refer more new customers to you, and will take more of your recommended products and/or services.

Having a relationship with your customers is HUGE, and the best way to have a business relationship with a large group of people is via a monthly newsletter that they can open and read. I want to make one more point before I move on: The act of sending a newsletter, by itself, will not provide you with the results and success you're looking for; you MUST get it opened and read to get results. It may seem like a no-brainer, but I often get newsletters from people who miss this point entirely.

No. 6 – Newsletters Help Build Your Brand

I am not normally a huge fan of building a brand. I have found that building a brand takes a ton of time and money, both things most small-business owners like us lack. But, as an added bonus, by publishing a monthly newsletter, you are getting many of the benefits of a brand in the mind of your customers. Obviously, having a brand has value—just ask Coca-Cola. But I prefer brand building to be a nice side benefit to my marketing, not a primary reason to do marketing.

No. 7 – Newsletters Have Staying Power

A good newsletter is unlike any other type of advertising if you do it right. People don't see the newsletter as an advertisement at all but instead as a publication, and you know what people do with publications? They keep them. Because newsletters are perceived as a publication, many people will have months of your newsletters just laying around. The U.S. Post Office did a study on all categories of direct mail and found newsletters have an average shelf life of four months in a home or business.

Recently, I had two experiences that support the U.S. Post Office study. The first was when I went to meet a long-time client for lunch. I ended up waiting for him in his office while he finished up with a patient, and while I was there, I saw five newsletters and a greeting card I had sent him, lingering in various spots on his desk.

Another time, I had a client tell me about a customer of his who loves his newsletter so much that she has made a binder just for his newsletters; she saves every issue. How would you like it if a customer or prospect enjoyed reading your publication so much, she saved every issue? When this customer needs more of my client's services, whom do you think she is going to call? Do you think this person is going to price shop my client, when she has kept every issue of his newsletter to date? Of course not. He has her as a customer, possibly for life.

The staying power of newsletters is massive and helps increase many of the areas I have already talked about (think referrals, the ability to sell more products and services to existing customers, branding, and so much more).

No. 8 – Newsletters Have Pass-Around Value

One of the things I love most about newsletters is their pass-around value. When you include valuable content in your newsletter, there's always the opportunity for people to give your newsletter to friends, family members, or associates to read. Of course, when they hand off your newsletter, they are also giving you an endorsement. A client of mine, Dr. Aldon Hilton, a dentist, recently told me about how his newsletter got passed around and the results.

A prospect of his had been getting his newsletter for months, and one day on the golf course, Dr. Hilton's prospect was hanging with a golfing buddy when they started talking about the golfing buddy's son. The son needed some dental work and wasn't sure where to go to get help for his specialized problem. Dr. Hilton's prospect remembered reading a story in the most recent newsletter and, after their golf game, went to his car to get the newsletter for his golfing buddy. The golfing buddy gave the newsletter to his son, who then made an appointment and ended up spending just over $8,000 with Dr. Hilton.

Had Dr. Hilton simply sent an ad to his prospect, there's no way that prospect would have kept the ad. Dr. Hilton's prospect would have said nothing to his golfing buddy, and that means the golfing buddy would have never told his son about Dr. Hilton. This is not an isolated story. I hear stories similar to this all the time. All you have to do to get your newsletter passed around is provide great value. Then, your customers and prospects will naturally share your publications with family and friends.

***

Newsletters have the power to grow your business, retain customers, and increase referrals. They maximize customer LTV, they ensure you stay top of mind with current customers and prospects, and they make it easier to sell to existing customers. They also increase your expert/celebrity status, build relationships, build your brand, stick around for a while, and have excellent pass-around value. And the best part is, you can get all of these benefits with a single monthly newsletter. No need to use six different strategies to get only one or two of the benefits we talked about.

For a quick exercise in math and to learn more about the power of retention, visit www.thenewsletterpro.com/book-resources to download your free Attrition Calculator and a copy of our Ultimate Guide to Customer Retention.

Now that you understand how powerful newsletters are, let's look into the mechanics of putting together a successful monthly newsletter.

CHAPTER 5

How to Create a Monthly Newsletter: The Planning Phase

When we first sign up a new client, we spend a lot of time planning their newsletter. We take a close look at who is going to be receiving the newsletter, and then we plan our content around that person.

Let me give you an example. One of our regular clients is a personal injury attorney who mails his newsletter to all the chiropractors in his area. The type of people who will be receiving the newsletter varies because we never know who in the office is going to read the newsletter before the doctor sees it. Also, we can't always be 100 percent sure who is giving out the referral: Is it the doctor, or is it the office manager?

What we do know is that the goal of the newsletter is for the doctors to read it, so we want to give them valuable information. In this scenario, during our planning and strategy session, we would want to make sure a portion of the newsletter is dedicated to content that will help the chiropractor grow or improve their practice. We would also want to endear the attorney to the chiropractor and their office staff, so they will want to send referrals to our client. Additionally, we would want to include a section with some fun in it, which likely will be for both the chiropractor and the office staff. (I'll share examples of both valuable content and fun article topics here soon—keep reading!)

At this point, we would estimate how much content those sections would require and then brainstorm for additional sections that would be appealing to our target audience.

Once we have an idea of the type of sections we are going to have, or have an estimate of how long each article will be, we double check that the sections we have created will be of interest to our target audience, which in this case, is the chiropractor and their office staff.

The scenario I used is an example of a B2B newsletter. Unfortunately, most of the B2B newsletters I've seen have been stuffy and boring. It's almost as if the people who are selling to other businesses actually believe they are selling *to the business* and not to the people who run it. Nothing could be further from the truth. Just like in B2C, at the end of the day, a person, not a business, buys the product. If you remember back to the start of the book, I told you the No. 1 sin of all of marketing was to be boring, and most B2B newsletters I see *are* boring. Whatever you do when creating your newsletter, remember to be engaging and original!

About a year ago, I had a client, who is also a friend of mine, who wanted to do newsletters. We were selling in a B2B market. We went through the process of planning his newsletter, and he and his wife reluctantly agreed to the nonbusiness content we suggested. As we started to produce the newsletter, he started removing more and more of the fun B2B content, asking us to replace it with very boring content that was all industry-specific information. This newsletter was quickly becoming a disaster, and I knew, before we ever printed a single issue, that in the long run, there was no way this newsletter was going to get the client his desired results. So, although he is a friend, I ended our business relationship. We have published a number of B2B newsletters over the years, and to this day, fun and interesting ones always outperform the boring ones for one simple fact—no one reads the boring newsletters.

At The Newsletter Pro, we have a specialized team of individuals whose entire job is dedicated to setting up new accounts and working with clients on the strategy of their newsletter. Don't take this lightly. Making the right choices and keeping the business content to no more than 25 percent of the newsletter will get you readership, which is what will get you results.

CHAPTER 6
Design and Layout

I am by no means a graphic designer, and I don't pretend to be one. But I do know both good and bad graphic design when I see it. Most newsletters fall in the bad graphic design category. Hopefully, with these tips, your newsletter will be interesting and appealing to the eye, and will encourage, rather than discourage, readership. Below are areas of graphic design that you will need to consider when working to publish a successful newsletter.

Color or Black and White (B&W)
You have heard the saying, "A picture is worth a thousand words," right?

Well, the full thousand words don't apply to B&W images. Your newsletter should be printed in color, because quite frankly, B&W newsletters are dull. At the end of the day, a B&W newsletter is better than no newsletter, but upgrade to color as soon as possible. It adds a level of quality to your newsletter that sets it apart as a professional publication.

Masthead and Footer

Your newsletter should have a unique masthead and coordinating footer. When having my graphic designers create a masthead and footer, I like to use colors similar to those on the client's website and/or logo. If you are not a graphic designer by trade, your masthead and footer need to be professionally created for you. Often, I see solid-colored boxes with the newsletter name on it and a logo dropped in; these are prime examples of poor or amateur graphic design.

Header Example:

Footer Example:

Name of the Newsletter

Typically, you want the name of your newsletter to be something other than your business name, unless your business name is descriptive of your service. For example, if you own West Village Dental, that shouldn't be the name of your newsletter. You may want to try something more

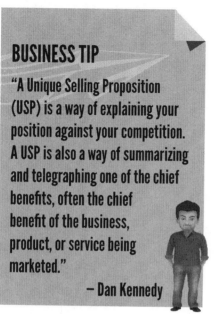

BUSINESS TIP

"A Unique Selling Proposition (USP) is a way of explaining your position against your competition. A USP is also a way of summarizing and telegraphing one of the chief benefits, often the chief benefit of the business, product, or service being marketed."

— Dan Kennedy

along the lines of "The Monthly Smile." Our newsletter is called "The Newsletter Pro" because we are the premier newsletter company.

Many of our clients get pretty creative with their newsletter names and use a play on words. We even had a client, a dentist, who loved his pets so much that part of his newsletter was written in the pets' voices. The client named his newsletter to reflect that: "The Doggone Dental Digest." Get creative. Be fun!

Newsletter Tagline

A tagline is a great place to highlight what makes you different. The reason a tagline is important is you never know who is going to end up with a copy of your newsletter, and you want them to be able to quickly understand what it is that you do and what makes you special. Many times, you can use your company's unique selling proposition (USP) as the tagline.

Newsletter Layout

Simply having everything in nice square boxes is not good graphic design and a little boring. When building your layout, you need to do more than make sure the text fits on the page. Consider how your readers' eyes move across the page. What do you want them to notice first? How will their experience flow from the imagery to the articles?

Inside Spread Layout Example:

Use of Pictures

As we talked about earlier, a picture is worth a thousand words, and you should use imagery as often as possible. One type of imagery that is often overlooked is the personal photo. Whenever you have the chance, you should include a personal or family picture to help build that relationship with people. If you don't have that, what about one of your pet or your favorite vacation spot? Don't forget—you never know what is going to resonate with someone.

Newsletter Length

A common question I get is how long should a newsletter be? For 90 percent of the business population, a four-page newsletter is the preferred length. Some business models can justify an eight-page newsletter. Typically, the people I see making the best use of an eight-page newsletter are the ones selling B2B or membership-based products, though high-volume retailers also benefit. Like anything, there are exceptions to the rules, but most people will be fine with a four-page newsletter.

Every now and again, I'm asked about a two-page newsletter. In virtually all cases, a two-page newsletter is just too small because you can't get enough content on the page to make it valuable— as you will see in the next chapter where I lay out for you what type of content you should have. There is almost NO WAY you can include enough content in just two pages to make it as valuable as it needs to be. Because of the smaller size, you may even find yourself tempted to only put in information about your business and industry so that you don't "waste" any valuable space. If you do that, though, you will quickly find yourself with a boring newsletter.

Looking for a newsletter template? We've got you covered.

Visit www.thenewsletterpro.com/book-resources to download your free copy. And while you're there, check out the other great resources we offer!

CHAPTER 7
Email or Print Newsletters

This far into the book, I am sure it is obvious that I am a print newsletter guy, because I have mentioned the words "print newsletter" multiple times. But I didn't come to that position without doing a little research, so here is what I found.

Email

Although email is "free," its deliverability rate is challenging. The average mass commercial email (such as an electronic newsletter) is estimated by major email players like Google and Yahoo to only make it to your prospects' inboxes between 16 and

60 percent of the time. Of course, you won't know what percentage of your customers actually receive your emails, let alone open and read them. If, for some reason, you want to reach only 16 to 60 percent of your clients this month, then maybe it's a good idea to do an e-newsletter. But if you want to reach closer to 100 percent of them, it is not going to happen with email.

A recent survey done by Marketing Sherpa found that the average read time on an email is between 15 and 20 seconds. WHAT!? You can't effectively build a relationship in 15 to 20 seconds a month. One reason for the fast readership rate is the infinite number of distractions on the internet. On their computers, your prospects are only a click away from Facebook, online video games, instant messages, and a bazillion other distractions. If all of that weren't bad enough, companies like Google have come up with new features like priority inbox, where they sort your emails by what they think you will be most interested in reading. This means that every month your customer doesn't read your emails, your content gets put into their inbox in a lower and lower position. Eventually, if they never open your emails, those emails won't even make it into their inboxes. Now that sucks.

The other challenge with an email newsletter is that the number of emails people receive per day is increasing drastically. A 2015 study found that the average American adult receives 147 emails per day. The new advice in email marketing is to email every day. Why? Because the response continues to decline with email marketing, so that you must promote daily to even get close to the same results you would have gotten promoting a few times a week five years ago.

Print

The single biggest negative to a print newsletter is the cost. A print newsletter is going to cost more than an email newsletter. As far as other negatives go, it is harder to print a newsletter and keep up with postal regulations. Those are the negatives, as far as I see them.

We have covered many of the positives of a print newsletter in this book so far, but let's list out a few of the benefits you'll get with the print newsletter that you will NOT get with an email newsletter.

- **Near 100 percent deliverability.** This by itself is worth the price of admission—your newsletter getting to EVERY client EVERY time!

- **Staying power.** The average email hangs around for seconds; a newsletter can literally hang around for months. Remember when I told you the story of the franchise I was researching and ultimately bought? I still have a binder full of their old newsletters. They were that interesting and that fun to read!

- **Brand building.** With a well-designed and branded newsletter, you are supporting your brand image with the consistency of print and making a physical connection that is impossible with email.

- **Consumption.** Studies have shown the average person will NOT consume most email newsletters. On the other hand, they do consume most of a print newsletter.

- **Increased referrals.** With readership of 15 to 20 seconds for the average email newsletter and less than 60 percent of people getting your e-publication, the average business sees no measurable increase in referrals from sending an email newsletter.

- **Pass-around value.** You may get your email newsletter forwarded, but in many instances, that forward is seen as spam. When I hand or mail you a print newsletter, you know it is not spam. You know that friends, family members, or neighbors have read this publication and thought of you. They are giving it to you for a reason. That would make me read it. What about you?

I could go on, but you get the point. Is an email newsletter better than nothing? Slightly, but it takes a massive amount of effort to publish a good newsletter each month. If you're going to invest all of that effort, you should get the maximum results.

A few days ago, I was sitting in a meeting with a lawyer who said he knows how valuable his newsletter is, but that he literally has to lock himself into a room for half a day to complete it. At his hourly rate, that is insane. But he knows the value of creating a good newsletter for his clients and referral sources, and he does it because a print newsletter makes a positive impact on his ability to maintain relationships with clients, naturally increasing retention and referrals. He wouldn't waste this effort on creating content for an e-newsletter that is likely to be lost to the black hole of email; he does it for the reliability of print.

Still not sure whether print trumps email? On your spouse's next birthday, just send him or her an e-greeting. Don't acknowledge his or her birthday in any other way. No real cards, no verbal acknowledgment, no gifts, no birthday nookie. Nothing but an e-card. If that goes over well for you, then by all means, send your newsletter via email.

With that said, let me give you a summary of my advice on this subject matter. The right answer here is do both print and email. The only time you should send emails only is when they're for a select portion of your list. For example, if you have a massive list—15,000-plus—and you have to decrease the mailing list size due to budget concerns, send the print newsletter to the people who have made a purchase recently and/or have made large purchases in the semi-recent past, and send the email newsletter to everyone else. If the above scenario doesn't describe you, send the newsletter in both formats.

BUSINESS TIP

"Never rely solely on email marketing. The most successful marketing strategy marries print and online media for a well-rounded, multi-channel campaign. In fact, 76 percent of small businesses state that their ideal marketing strategy encompasses a combination of both print and digital communication to increase conversions."

— Pitney Bowes, 2015

CHAPTER 8

Creating Content for Your Newsletter

Creating content is the toughest part of publishing a monthly newsletter. Most people stare at a blank page and have a very hard time going from nothing to something. I fully understand. My company creates hundreds of unique newsletters every month, and even for our professional writers, it can be difficult at times. Below are some ideas for content and how to use them to help you go from a blank page to a finished newsletter.

Personal Articles

Personal articles are the single most important element to having a successful newsletter, and they should be the easiest to write since they are about you, your life, your business, and your family. These articles represent the relationship-building aspect of your newsletter.

People struggle with these articles in three places.

1. People feel that their lives aren't newsworthy, and therefore won't hold a reader's attention. That couldn't be further from the truth. Most of us do something unique or exciting, or we have something unusual happen to us. Maybe you just got back from a fun vacation. Or maybe you recently welcomed a new member to the family. We are all guilty of thinking our lives are boring and everyone else's lives are more exciting. Give your customers a bit of personal information, and you'll be surprised at how they connect with you and share similar personal stories from their lives.

2. The next concern I see people struggling with is their privacy. You don't need to share your innermost thoughts in the newsletter, and sharing information about your most recent vacation or talking about your love for NCAA football is not a breach of national security. If it's on Facebook, it's not really that personal. Likely, anyone who knows you even a little already knows these details about you.

   I have to be honest. I have struggled with this from time to time myself. The most difficult and personal article I have ever put in my own newsletter was titled "He Stopped Breathing for 3½ Minutes," accompanied by a picture of my almost 3-year-old son, Jeremiah. I wrote the article a few days before his third birthday, and it tells the story of how Jeremiah stopped breathing for three-and-a-half minutes a few days before his first birthday. To be honest, when I was writing the story, it was so personal, it made me tear up. I tried to write other articles for the newsletter, but I simply couldn't. He was what was on my mind that month. I published the article and received a huge response. Numerous people shared experiences they'd had that were similar to mine, while others told me they'd teared up reading it.

At the end of the day, some people may have read that story and thought I was using my son, but that wasn't it at all. He and that situation were on my mind, and I decided to share the story. I have included a copy of this, plus two other examples of personal articles I have used in my newsletters, at the end of this chapter.

3. People struggle with giving enough information. When I review some of the newsletters we create for clients, I sometimes see personal articles that are two or three paragraphs long that don't really say much. Typically, when I see this, I go in and talk to our writers because for almost all of our customers, we interview them and then ghost write the articles. Our conversations go something like this:

Me: Why is this article so short?

Writer: The client was short on time this month and only gave me a little bit of information.

Me: Did you tell them this wasn't going to be enough information to write a full article and ask to reschedule?

Writer: Yup, they said it was okay if it was short this month.

Me: Okay, but let me know if they try to put in a short article again next month.

These articles are SO important. Without these personal articles, it takes much longer to build those vital relationships with your clients and prospects. Some clients will never feel any connection to you without the personal article.

One of the primary goals of your newsletter is to let people get to know you so they feel connected to you. People do business with people they know and like. If you are not prepared to let people in, even a little bit, newsletters are likely not for you.

Fun Pieces

All newsletters need an element of fun in them. These pieces can be in a mix of content and can change on a regular basis, if you want. Below is a list of ideas of fun content you may want to include in your newsletter:

- Sudoku puzzles
- Crossword puzzles
- Jokes
- Funny pictures
- Funny stories
- Contests

Any combination of these will help increase readership and engagement with your newsletter. If you're still having issues figuring out what type of fun stuff people want to read, subscribe to *Reader's Digest*.

Here are some other popular article types and ideas:

- Top 10 lists

- Recipes (the most popular category of books sold in book stores)

- How-to articles

- Tips on parenting

- Vacation ideas

- Technology tips

- Time management ideas

- Luxury items

Both the fun section and these other articles would be considered nonrelevant content. This nonrelevant content is very important because it increases readership of the overall newsletter. Nothing is worse than sending a newsletter that no one reads. Not only have you wasted your money, but more importantly, you have wasted your time. Having a good mix of relevant content (content that is about your industry), nonrelevant content, and personal information is what is going to make your newsletter great.

* * *

Example Cover Article From "The Newsletter Pro" Monthly Print Newsletter:

He Stopped Breathing for 3½ Minutes

On July 16, my son Jeremiah turned 3 years old. It was a day he had been looking forward to since my other son Tyler had turned 6 in January. Every year around Jeremiah's birthday, I take a moment and thank the Lord for another year with him because there was a time I wasn't sure he would live to see his first birthday—much less his third.

When Jeremiah was born, we knew right away that something was wrong with him. The gasping and grunting sounds he exerted while doing minor things we all take for granted (like breathing) were just not what you expect to hear from a brand new beautiful gift from God. As a parent, it is so very hard to see your kid sick or in pain. It is even harder to not know what is causing the problems.

After just under a year of struggling to find out what was wrong with Jeremiah, we were told he had severe sleep apnea. We scheduled an appointment to have a sleep study conducted. They hooked Jeremiah up to more probes and monitors than I thought they could physically fit on a baby (but they managed). These probes were monitoring everything—brain activity, the number of times he stopped breathing per hour, and everything in between. As they were hooking Jeremiah up, we noticed he had a slight fever and asked if that would affect the sleep study. The nurse told us it wouldn't, and they continued hooking him up.

The room at this sleep center is set up so the parents have one room and the baby has an adjoining room. My wife, Mariah, and I decided she would stay the night with Jeremiah so I could go home and be with our other kids.

As the night went on and Mariah was just getting ready to doze off, she heard an alarming amount of noise coming from Jeremiah's room. She ran in to find him having a seizure. She screamed for the nurse, and the next thing she heard is every parent's worst nightmare—a droning tone from the monitor, indicating that Jeremiah was flatlining.

They called 911 for an ambulance and tried to resuscitate him. As the monitor continued to go off, fear and panic set in, and time started to slow down. The feeling of helplessness was almost unbearable. After what felt to Mariah like an eternity, another minute ticked by. The monitors were still blaring, and the nurses continued to try to bring our baby boy back to life. Three minutes had passed, and still nothing. As a parent, you can only imagine the worst. You are literally begging God to save your child.

Finally, at three minutes and just over 30 seconds, baby Jeremiah took one shallow breath and then slowly another, and another. As he was loaded into the ambulance, Mariah (still in shock) called me and said, "Jeremiah had a seizure and stopped breathing for three-and-a-half minutes. We are in an ambulance on our way to St. Al's downtown; I have to go" and hung up. I had NEVER moved so fast getting out of my house, nor had I ever driven that fast down the freeway before. The whole time I did not know if my son was dead or alive. Tears were streaming down my cheeks, and I was praying that I hadn't lost him. I made it to the hospital to find that Jeremiah was, in fact, alive. There are no words to describe how relieved I was. He had numerous ER doctors all around him, and he was very disoriented, to say the least. I hugged and comforted my wife and waited for the doctors to finish.

We ultimately found out he had had a fibral seizure, which happens in about 20 percent of kids under 5 years old. The additional good news was that by the time he turned 5, he would no longer be at risk for these seizures. We asked if he would experience any permanent damage from the three-and-a-half minutes of not breathing or the seizure, and, thankfully, the answer was no. Brain damage doesn't set in until after four minutes of not breathing. Jeremiah ultimately had a few surgeries to fix the breathing issues and is now a happy and healthy 3-year-old.

That day changed me both personally and professionally forever. As much as I enjoy working, and I do, I realized that on my death bed, I am not going to look back and say, "If I had only worked those few extra days, my life would be complete." In fact I believe it will be the opposite. I am much more likely to look back and say, "I should have spent more time with the people that mattered most to me."

I personally enjoy working and really don't see a day even in my distant future where I won't work at least a little, but it is important to find a good balance and make sure that every day you take a little time for those people in your life who really matter. At the end of this life, nothing else is going to seem more important.

Shaun Buck

P.S. Do me a favor. When you get home today, kiss all the little (or big) Jeremiahs that you have running around.

***

Example Cover Article From "The Newsletter Pro" Monthly Print Newsletter:

The Journey From Entrepreneur to Chief Executive Officer

Every now and again, I enjoy spending a little time reflecting on where I am and where I have come from. For me, one of the most major changes has been from entrepreneur to chief executive officer. As an entrepreneur, over the last several years I've been very interested in growth—and not just any growth, but fast growth. From 2011–2014 The Newsletter Pro has grown by just under 3,000 percent. As the saying goes, "I feel the need...the need for speed" (Maverick and Goose, *Top Gun*). About a year ago, my team (and my entrepreneurial self) made the decision that we wanted to be the largest print newsletter company in the world. We did a bit of research and estimated if we were mailing 1 million pieces of mail per month, we would easily hit our goal. That BHAG (Big Hairy Audacious Goal) set us down a path that has been one of the most challenging in my professional career.

I didn't know this at the time, but to hit our goal, I was going to have to make major changes to who I am and the way I manage and run a business. I was going to have to adjust some of my thinking and leadership style from a "shoot from the hip" entrepreneur to a CEO and manager of managers. On this journey (of which I am still firmly in the middle) I have had to realize my shortcomings and adjust a ton. Here is a brief list of my findings:

- I am likely the reason for the delay.

- I can't do it all.

- I can't approve it all.

- I don't know it all.

- There are people who can do it better than I can.

- There is a give and take with all relationships.

- Sometimes others have to win (or at a minimum, be heard).

- I need to take on tasks and projects others can do.

- I do not have to be the last person to leave the office.

- My team wants us to succeed, and if I get out of the way and trust them, they can do great things.

- The mission and vision are bigger than any single person (including me).

- Systems rule!

- Slow and steady changes win the race. And the bigger you get, the more that is true.

- I am the investor in this business and need to operate as such.

- Culture matters.

- Your team matters.

When I first started out, the business revolved around me, but as we have grown, I have had to realize that there is no "I" in The Newsletter Pro.

Not too long ago, I sat down by myself and looked at all the changes the company and I were going through. I then considered all the changes we likely will have to go through in the future. The purpose of this was to decide if all this change was what I wanted for my business and my life. I feel it is a question not enough people ask. The decision wasn't easy, mainly because changing is hard. Ultimately I decided that growing and changing is exactly what I want. I want to grow as an entrepreneur and ultimately into a successful CEO.

A word of caution for those who don't want to change:

I have watched a few companies—clients of The Newsletter Pro—come and go because the entrepreneurs have decided to fight against being CEOs. These entrepreneurs either don't realize they need to change or they simply don't want to. There comes a point where you MUST make the change or you will have to be okay with and happy with your business where it is presently. A good rule of thumb is between the 2-million and 4-million mark in sales. If you don't start to transition from entrepreneur to CEO, but still insist on growing, as with the majority of businesses, yours will likely turn from something that is fun and exciting to something that is a constant struggle and not enjoyable.

I'm watching a Red Alert Client (our code name for someone who is likely going to cancel our service) right now. This client is super smart and successful. From what I can tell, he is an amazing provider for his service. My guess is he is doing between 2.5 million and 3 million in revenue, but he can't let go. Because of that, his business is likely in some of degree of stagnation, decline, or at a minimum, he is (or soon will be) miserable. This client must stamp his approval on everything at every turn. He doesn't even trust his own team. My guess is he won't be a client much longer. Of course we have identified that he is in our "danger zone" and will work to help him, but my experience tells me that it is a 50/50 chance he survives as a client. There is just no way he can stamp his approval on every area of his business, as well as the newsletter, given how busy he is. Ultimately he will decide to let it go or he will quit. If he quits, it will be both our loss and his.

As an entrepreneur or CEO, our job is to make the hard decisions; our job is to improve and change both ourselves and our business. There will be a point where you have to decide if the sacrifice is worth it or not. For me and my team, I have decided even though the journey is and has been difficult, the destination is worth the sacrifice.

Shaun Buck

***

Example Cover Article From "The Newsletter Pro" Monthly Print Newsletter:

What Are You Willing to Give Up?

I met my wife, Mariah, 15 years ago, and nearly that entire time there has been just one thing she has wanted to do: be a stay-at-home mom. Fortunately, over the past 12 years, we have been in a position for her to do just that. The only exceptions being when I needed her help with one of the many businesses we have owned over the last decade.

When we first met, she thought the idea of being a business owner was strange. She didn't understand why I spent so much time reading and studying about business, and for the life of her, she couldn't figure out why in the world I was so interested in what a grumpy man named Dan Kennedy, who was sitting on a bull, had to say.

Much has changed over the last 15 years; my wife no longer wonders why I read and study business so much; she understands why I cling to every word Dan Kennedy has to say; and she has even decided he is not all that grumpy. In fact, she now rather enjoys business, and a few weeks ago, she even came to me to talk about her starting her own.

I was a bit confused at first. After all, her stated dream was to be a stay-at-home mom…and she is. We don't "need" the extra money—long gone are the days when we couldn't afford groceries toward the end of the month. My business, and in turn, her business, is already successful, so my big question was, "Why do you want to start a business?"

She and I discussed the idea a few times over the following weeks—the pros and cons, how to market, and the time commitment that would be required. After a few days, we had an outline and a basic plan etched out. We wanted to make sure this decision was right for both her and our family. As we went back and forth, I finally said, "There's really only one question you need to answer to make this decision: 'What are you willing to give up in order to own this business?' "

There is a cost to everything we do. I have heard on more than one occasion how lucky I am that my business has grown so much and done so well in a relatively short period of time, but that statement discounts the fact that I have been full-time, self-employed since 2000—not to mention the thousands of hours I've spent studying business and marketing, or the hundreds of thousands of dollars I've spent on my education. It would be like meeting a doctor and telling them they are so lucky to have become a doctor. To get to where I am today, I had to give up partying in my 20s, spending time with my family, having the "security" that is provided by a real job, and a massive amount of treasure.

Right now I am making some of those same sacrifices to grow The Newsletter Pro. I have to travel 10-14 times per year, which is something I never thought I would have to do. While I enjoy exhibiting and speaking at trade shows, it oftentimes means that I miss something equally as important, like my son's football games, or a family event. It's not uncommon for me to be at work before my family even wakes up, and on many occasions, I don't make it home until they've already gone to bed. In all honesty, on many of those evenings, it would be far easier (and far more enjoyable) to simply sit down with my kids and watch TV.

I am not giving you these examples for any reason other than to prove my point; life and business is about choices. If you want to make $10,000 per month, what are you willing to give up to have that? If you want a multimillion-dollar business, you will likely have to give up even more to get there. If you want to be an overnight success, it is going to take a lot of study, hard work, and likely a number of years.

In the end, Mariah decided that she wasn't willing to give up what was required of her to own this new business. Some of you might view that decision as a failure, or "quitting before you even start," but I disagree. I have found time and time again that real happiness and long-term prosperity in life comes from knowing which opportunities to pass on and which opportunities to say yes to.

Shaun Buck

CHAPTER 9

The Top 6 Mistakes People Make When Publishing Their Newsletters

I get to see a ton of self-published newsletters. Because of that, I have seen more than a few mistakes. Here is a list of the top six mistakes I see most often with self-published newsletters. I decided to put these in order of how detrimental these mistakes are to achieving your goals.

Mistake No. 1 – Not Publishing Monthly

This is, by far, the biggest mistake people make. When you don't publish monthly, you lose most of the benefits you get from publishing a newsletter.

Let me give you some examples. One of the benefits you are trying to achieve with your newsletter is building a relationship. How much of a relationship can you build if you are talking to your customers only every few months? The answer is no relationship. When you mail only every few months, people can't remember the last time they got your newsletter or whether they even liked it the last time they got it. Heck, they may not even remember who you are, let alone feel they have any relationship with you.

Think about it like this: How often do you communicate with people you like and have a relationship with? Of course, there are some people you talk to more often and others less often, but few people have a real relationship with the individuals they talk to only once every few months. Let me give you an example. If I have not talked to my dad on the phone in more than four or five days, I may get a voicemail from him asking me if everything is okay. Our relationship is such that, if he has not heard from me in a relatively short time, he starts to wonder whether everything is okay. On the other hand, I have some "friends," who truly used to be my friends a decade ago, whom I speak with only every three to 12 months. At this point, we aren't really friends anymore. Typically, when one of us calls, it is because we need something or are bored, waiting for a plane or are driving some long distance and have run out of other people to call. There is no relationship there. We have some familiarity, but we don't have a relationship.

What kind of relationship do you want to have with your customers, referral sources, or prospects? If your customers aren't very important to you and you don't want more referrals, by all means, send quarterly. Otherwise, you have to send monthly. Keep that close relationship with them.

Note: I know I was laying it on a bit thick in the last paragraph. I also know your customers are important to you. Without them, you wouldn't be in business. Of course I understand that. The reason I laid it on so thick was because I see too many people take their customers for granted and then wonder why business is down or patients don't take recommended treatments. I know it can be scary at first, mailing monthly, but it is the only way to get the results you want and need.

Mistake No. 2 – Being Boring

I see boring newsletters a lot. All industries publish them, but the one that gets mailed to my house happens to be a dental newsletter. Each month, this stock newsletter talks all about teeth and gum disease. I cringe every time it comes in the mail. The last thing in the world I would ever want to read is a newsletter about gum disease. And to add insult to injury, they include pictures in this newsletter. Seriously, no one—not even a dental student—wants to read about or see pictures of someone's rotting gums. The funny thing is, according to a report reviewed by Columbia University College of Dental Medicine, an estimated 30 million to 40 million Americans have at least a minor fear of the dentist. Who in their right mind thought it would be a good idea to mail a monthly newsletter about dental horrors to a population of people who likely have a mild fear of the dentist? That would be like Delta airlines sending out a monthly newsletter describing airplane crashes and close calls to people who are scared of flying. It's just nuts. My estimates are that boring newsletters have less than a 10 percent readership rate and less than a 2 percent cover-to-cover readership. What a waste of time and money! If you are a dentist mailing a newsletter like this, STOP IT!

Note: I know my estimates are not scientific, but they are based on a survey I did on readership of a boring newsletter.

The moral of the story is, don't mail a boring newsletter just for the sake of mailing a newsletter. And if you're looking for a second moral, here it is: Don't mail a newsletter that will scare people. That simply isn't good business.

At the end of the day, it's far more fun and profitable to take half of the money you would have spent on creating, printing, and mailing a boring newsletter, and to simply light that money on fire. After that, you can take the other half of the money and have a fun night out on the town. You will get more bang for your buck doing that than you will sending out a boring newsletter.

Mistake No. 3 – Not Mailing to the Whole List

I am surprised by how often people ask me to whom they should be mailing. The answer to this question should be obvious to anyone who wants to grow their business:

- Anyone you want to do more business with in the future

- Anyone you want to send you a referral

- Anyone who has expressed an interest in your business but has not yet bought from you

When you look at that list, who would you want to cut out? But I see people cut people from that list all the time.

The person on the above list least likely to receive a newsletter is the person who has not yet bought something from you. As I shared with you at the start of this book, this is the one person you for sure want to mail to on a regular basis. That's how the dry cleaning franchisee sold me on buying a franchise, and if you follow up with your prospects, you will also close more deals. Let me share another story with you.

Just recently I received a call from a guy I had met nearly two years ago. He said he was ready to work with us and get his monthly newsletter out. He actually thanked me for mailing my newsletter to him each month. He said it had been a goal of his to get his monthly newsletter out and that, if I had not mailed my newsletter to him each month (for 20 months!), he never would have remembered who we were.

When we meet prospective clients, we put them on our mailing list for a minimum of one year. I have found that people are ready to buy when they are ready to buy, and for the most part, you are not going to rush them into a buying decision. But if you have kept in touch, when they are ready to buy, they'll think of you. They're not going to think of all of your competitors—businesses they haven't heard from—they're going to think of you, the person who has been following up with them for months.

If you have a group of people who naturally should be referring to you, they need to get a monthly newsletter from you. Here are some examples of natural referral sources:

- Personal injury attorneys can get referrals from chiropractors

- Oral surgeons can get referrals from general dentists

- Estate and trust lawyers can get referrals from accountants

Even if a company has never sent you a referral, you can add them to your newsletter cold list, and over time, some

Building Relationships That Matter. Personal. Professional. Powerful.

of those cold leads will start sending you referrals. At the beginning of the year, one of our personal injury attorneys told me that since he had started cold mailing his newsletter to chiropractors in his area, the number of referrals he has gotten from them has doubled. Not too bad if you ask me (and we'll talk about mailing to cold lists in just a bit).

Finally comes the idea of mailing to anyone you want to do business with in the future. This is where the list can get really big. As a rule of thumb, if people haven't done business with you within the past 12 to 24 months, they likely shouldn't be on this list. Of course, some businesses with a very high average customer lifetime value (LTV) may mail longer, and some with lower LTV, may mail for a shorter period of time, but as a general rule, 1 to 2 years works.

Mistake No. 4 – Poor Design

I have seen newsletters published by large companies that appear to have been designed by the boss's 8-year-old on Microsoft Paint. Your newsletter should match the image you are trying to convey. If your image is "we are a very small mom and pop company," by all means, do it yourself. If your image is "we are a professional company," your newsletter also needs to look professional. You wouldn't hand a new client one of those free business cards you got from VistaPrint that has the ad for VistaPrint on the back of it, would you? What about handing out business cards that are printed from your home Inkjet printer and have the perforated edges that scream, "I printed these at home and have no money"? Are you going to hand those out? Of course not. So don't create a newsletter that looks the same way. Unless you are a graphic designer and have been paid to do graphic design work by more than a dozen people in the past, don't try to lay out your own newsletter. It's simply not worth it.

Mistake No. 5 – Giving Up Too Soon!

Newsletters are not a get-rich-quick scheme. Customers are not going to come flooding in through your front door after reading the first issue. In reality, it takes somewhere between six to 12 months for your business to realize all of the benefits a newsletter provides. Before you go into publishing a newsletter, you need to understand it takes time to build readership; it takes time to build trust in that relationship; and it takes time to see results. Of course, I can tell you stories of people who have seen massive results much sooner, but don't go in banking on massive results from day one, because you will be disappointed. You should think of your newsletter as a long-term investment, not a quick flip for a profit. The ROI is built over time in the form of referrals and increased retention (leading to greater LTV). That's the truth.

Mistake No. 6 – Allowing Other People to Advertise in Your Newsletter

I have never understood the idea of allowing other people to put a blatant ad inside your newsletter. To be honest, this isn't a mistake I see as often as the other five mistakes, but I am always baffled when I do. Ads for other people's products and services, as a rule, should not be allowed. If you are going to violate the sanctity of your newsletter, at least do it for your own benefit.

If you do allow someone to make an offer in the newsletter, it needs to be in a ghostwritten guest column, signed by you, with a soft call to action at the end. The article needs to be targeted and beneficial to your reader, not just a sales piece. To the right is an example of an article where I allowed a guest writer to ghostwrite an article from my perspective. Use this article as an example of what a "guest column" should look like for your newsletter.

***

Example Guest Article From "The Newsletter Pro" Monthly Print Newsletter:

The Great Schlitz Beer Rescue: How a Simple Idea Saved Schlitz Beer

Schlitz Beer was locked in a death struggle. The brewery was mired in fifth place, and the competition was growing fiercer by the day. Breweries were pounding each other with more and more expensive ads. Bigger type, more pages. All shouting that their beer was THE PUREST!

When the water level rises like this, it's the companies a few rungs down from the top that drown, and the makers of Schlitz sensed that they were in serious trouble.

Desperate to cut through the noise, they made a wise move. They brought in an outside expert, a successful advertiser known for his ability to make products fly off the shelves.

The ad man didn't waste any time. He immediately asked for a tour of the brewery, and what he saw stunned him.

Plate-glass rooms full of filtered air, designed to cool the beer without contaminating it. The original mother yeast cell—developed by the brewery after 1,200 experiments— that all of the yeast in Schlitz beer descended from. Four- thousand-foot deep artesian wells drilled to where the water was purest.

After the tour, he turned to the brewers and asked, "Why on earth aren't you telling anyone about this?"

"It's nothing special," the brewers said. "All the brewers do these things."

That was true—but the public had no idea because none of the brewers talked about it in their advertising.

So the ad man rolled up his sleeves and wrote a series of ads describing the painstaking lengths the brewery went through to ensure the purity of its beer.

Did the campaign work?

Well, when the ads rolled out, demand for Schlitz Beer skyrocketed. And within months, Schlitz jumped from a mediocre fifth place to slugging it out for first.

All because an outsider saw what the brewers couldn't. For me, it's pretty easy to hear a story like that and come down hard on the brewers. How could they be so blind?

But if I'm honest with myself, I can think of countless times where I've missed opportunities that were so obvious that you'd think an 8-year-old could see them.

This old saying sums it up:

"It's hard to read the label when you're inside the bottle."

Whatever you're doing, whether it's deciding on your next new product or service, or writing an article or an ad to promote your business, or deciding which strategy or opportunity deserves your focus…don't assume that you see everything.

It's impossible to look at what you're doing objectively. You will always have blind spots.

Sometimes it's because you just really fall in love with an idea and forget to do a sanity check to find out what your customers think about it.

Other times, you've been working on something for so long that you lose perspective. Everything about it seems awful and you can't stand to think about it anymore.

That's why—no matter where you are in your business—one of the most valuable things you can do is get an outside perspective.

When you put fresh eyeballs on your business, "obvious" things that you'd never see on your own become visible.

In my business, many of my biggest breakthroughs came from master direct marketer Dan Kennedy, and the people I've met through his organization.

Dan has a knack for looking at a situation and zeroing in like a laser on the ONE thing that makes all the difference.

True masters can do that. They'll give you a single sentence—short enough to fit on an index card—that's worth tens of thousands of dollars to your business.

I've had this same experience from studying at the feet of masters whom I've never met.

Great copywriters like Robert Collier, John Caples, Eugene Schwartz, and even the genius behind the Schlitz Beer turnaround, the legendary Claude Hopkins.

These guys have more than a century of combined experience selling everything from trainloads of coal to spark plugs and memory aids. Any business problem you can think of, they've solved it a dozen times over.

Recently I discovered a tool that helps me look at my own writing through the eyes of Collier, Caples, Schwartz, and Hopkins.

It was created by a friend of mine, Richard Boureston. Richard is a copywriter and fellow student of direct marketing, and he's spent more than 10 years studying these masters.

What he's done is distill their 100+ years of marketing and copywriting wisdom down into a deck of 115 cards that you can hold in one hand—and review in just minutes.

Here's how you use this tool...

When you're sitting down at your keyboard, you spend a minute thinking about your audience and your product. Then you pick up the deck and start to flick through the cards, letting your eyes absorb the pithy wisdom of the advertising masters.

And then—BAM! Something clicks and you're looking at your business from a whole new perspective.

This deck of cards is like masterminding with the greatest advertising minds in history.

I highly recommend checking it out. And the best part is, Richard is actually giving away this useful tool for free (if you'll help him out by paying for the shipping).

Grab yours here today: ConversionCatapult.com

Shaun

The Great Schlitz Beer Rescue
How a Simple Idea Saved Schlitz Beer

Schlitz Beer was locked in a death struggle. The brewery was mired in fifth place, and the competition was growing fiercer by the day. Breweries were pounding each other with more and more expensive ads. Bigger type, more pages. All shouting that their beer was THE PUREST!

When the water level rises like this, it's the companies a few rungs down from the top that drown, and the makers of Schlitz sensed that they were in serious trouble.

Desperate to cut through the noise, they made a wise move. They brought in an outside expert, a successful advertiser known for his ability to make products fly off the shelves.

The ad man didn't waste any time. He immediately asked for a tour of the brewery, and what he saw stunned him.

Plate-glass rooms full of filtered air, designed to cool the beer without contaminating it. The original mother yeast cell — developed by the brewery after 1,200 experiments — that all of the yeast in Schlitz beer descended from. Four-thousand-foot deep artesian wells drilled to where the water was purest.

After the tour, he turned to the brewers and asked, "Why on earth aren't you telling anyone about this?"

"It's nothing special," the brewers said. "All the brewers do these things."

That was true — but the public had no idea because none of the brewers talked about it in their advertising.

So the ad man rolled up his sleeves and wrote a series of ads describing the painstaking lengths the brewery went through to ensure the purity of its beer.

Did the campaign work?

Well, when the ads rolled out, demand for Schlitz Beer skyrocketed. And within months, Schlitz jumped from a mediocre fifth place to slugging it out for first.

All because an outsider saw what the brewers couldn't. For me, it's pretty easy to hear a story like that and come down hard on the brewers. How could they be so blind?

But if I'm honest with myself, I can think of countless times where I've missed opportunities that were so obvious that you'd think an 8-year-old could see them.

This old saying sums it up:

"It's hard to read the label when you're inside the bottle."

Whatever you're doing, whether it's deciding on your next new product or service, or writing an article or an ad to promote your business, or deciding which strategy or opportunity deserves your focus ... don't assume that you see everything.

It's impossible to look at what you're doing objectively. You will always have blind spots.

Sometimes it's because you just really fall in love with an idea and forget to do a sanity check to find out what your customers think about it.

Other times, you've been working on something for so long that you lose perspective. Everything about it seems awful and you can't stand to think about it anymore.

That's why — no matter where you are in your business — one of the most valuable things you can do is get an outside perspective.

When you put fresh eyeballs on your business, "obvious" things that you'd never see on your own become visible.

In my business, many of my biggest breakthroughs came from master direct marketer Dan Kennedy, and the people I've met through his organization.

Dan has a knack for looking at a situation and zeroing in like a laser on the ONE thing that makes all the difference.

True masters can do that. They'll give you a single sentence — short enough to fit on an index card — that's worth tens of thousands of dollars to your business.

I've had this same experience from studying at the feet of masters whom I've never met.

Great copywriters like Robert Collier, John Caples, Eugene Schwartz, and even the genius behind the Schlitz Beer turnaround, the legendary Claude Hopkins.

These guys have more than a century of combined experience selling everything from trainloads of coal to spark plugs and memory aids. Any business problem you can think of, they've solved it a dozen times over.

Recently I discovered a tool that helps me look at

my own writing through the eyes of Collier, Caples, Schwartz, and Hopkins.

It was created by a friend of mine, Richard Boureston. Richard is a copywriter and fellow student of direct marketing, and he's spent more than 10 years studying these masters.

What he's done is distill their 100+ years of marketing and copywriting wisdom down into a deck of 115 cards that you can hold in one hand — and review in just minutes.

Here's how you use this tool ...

When you're sitting down at your keyboard, you spend a minute thinking about your audience and your product. Then you pick up the deck and start to flick through the cards, letting your eyes absorb the pithy wisdom of the advertising masters.

And then — BAM! Something clicks and you're looking at your business from a whole new perspective.

This deck of cards is like masterminding with the greatest advertising minds in history.

I highly recommend checking it out. And the best part is, Richard is actually giving away this useful tool for free (if you'll help him out by paying for the shipping).

Grab yours here today: ConversionCatapult.com

–Shaun

CHAPTER 10

5 Ways to Use a Newsletter to Grow Your Business

Idea No. 1 – Cold Mail Your Newsletter

This idea is by no means new or unique to me, but it works. Find a list of people who are ideal for your product or service, and add each and every one of them to your monthly newsletter. We have seen this work in a number of industries. One of my favorite stories is one of a Realtor we mail for. She sends a very fun and interesting newsletter to every homeowner in the neighborhoods for which she would like to be the Realtor of choice. The average price of a home in the neighborhoods she mails to is between $250,000 and $300,000. On her third mailing, she listed not one, but two houses in one of her neighborhoods. The commission for those two houses alone has given her more than enough money to cover her newsletter for years to come. And another bonus—she is now seen as the choice Realtor for that neighborhood.

As I mentioned earlier, if you have a group of people who would make great referral sources, they should all be getting a newsletter from you. If you are going to be sending to a large group of people—for example, a personal injury attorney who is mailing to all the chiropractors in his area—then you want to have a separate newsletter just for them. In the chiropractors' newsletter, you should have all of the elements we talked about earlier (a personal article and some fun content). But in the sections where you may have put in an interesting nonrelevant article, you should instead insert information that will help your clients and/or prospects grow *their* business or improve their practice or quality of life. Since you are mailing to referral sources, you can typically afford to spend more per piece that is mailed out because you will be able to see direct business typically much sooner from this type of newsletter.

We have found that the addition of a monthly CD that helps the client grow their business, increases the number of clients who give referrals. Another great addition is a staff newsletter. This newsletter should help the client's support team do their jobs better, and it should have a ton of fun and interesting content in it.

Cold newsletter mailing is a great way to generate new leads and business from your newsletter. Whom can you cold mail a newsletter to who can refer new business to your company?

Since the first publication of this book, I've gotten a ton of questions about this strategy. This is more of an advanced strategy that works best for established businesses because it takes time to build relationships. This cold mailer strategy is more of a long-term strategy, less of a quick hit. Think about it like this: When you're just starting your business, you need to be more like a day trader, where money is returning itself quickly, and less Warren Buffet, where you are okay waiting for the return on investment. I would still suggest you mail a newsletter to prospects and customers who will absolutely return big for your business, but if you are just starting out, or are still on the smaller side, hold off on buying a list and mailing newsletters cold until you can justify a long-term investment in a project like that.

BUSINESS TIP

Sometimes you will need a list to get all the names and addresses of people you want to cold mail to. A good source for lists is www.NextMark.com. One word of caution: Most of their lists are one-time use only, so make sure you check on how many times you can mail to the list you bought so you don't run afoul of the list broker.

Idea No. 2 – Mail to Prospects and Include an Offer

This one is a no-brainer (but for prospects *only*). I know I just told you in Mistake No. 6 (Chapter 9) that using your newsletter to advertise for others is the worst thing you can do, but when you're mailing to your prospects, it's okay to occasionally include an offer for your product or service. Make it a newsletter-exclusive deal—one they can't get anywhere else. Even better, make it irresistible. Try to convert some of these prospects into customers.

My preferred method of making an offer is via a free-standing insert (FSI). The FSI can be all advertising. You don't need to include any real content in it, and it allows you to be more sales-focused while still preserving the sanctity of the newsletter because it's a separate insert and not attached to your main publication.

Another great way to use an FSI in a newsletter is for list segmentation. List segmentation is a book in and of itself, but you can use it to offer free reports, white papers, CDs, etc. to select audiences. That means you can send certain offers to the people who would be most interested in them. For example, if you are a dentist and you put an offer on an FSI for a report on veneers, and 11 patients opt in to get that free report, wouldn't it be a good idea to send them some additional information on veneers? Maybe even make them an offer? A veneer patient can spend anywhere from $15,000 to $25,000 on treatment. If you knew 11 people from your practice who were very interested in veneers, couldn't you afford to spend $200 on each of them to get one or two of them to pull the trigger? Of course you could. Using an FSI to segment your list so you can make direct offers to people who are interested in specific products and services you provide is smart business.

Idea No. 3 – Distribute Copies of Your Newsletter to Other Businesses That Have Similar Customers and/or Waiting Rooms

This is a simple but effective idea for people who are looking to meet clients who frequent nearby businesses. Go talk to the business owner, and ask them if you can leave copies of your newsletter in their office for their customers to read. If your ideal clients are sitting in waiting rooms, this is a no-brainer for both you and the business owners because they get free content that helps keep their customers entertained, and you get the chance to put yourself in front of prospective customers. If a business owner doesn't have a waiting room, ask if you can leave a small stand and free copies of your newsletter near the cash register where their customers check out or someplace else that makes sense.

When you use this strategy, it is a good idea to have some kind of lead generation call to action in the newsletter. For example, offer a free report with the top seven things you must know before you buy a new car. This way the newsletter doesn't come across to business owners as just another advertisement. Business owners will be more inclined to allow you to put your newsletter in their place of business if it isn't chock-full of coupons, but instead offers valuable content and helpful information.

A great example of a company that has created a whole franchise system from placing newsletters in businesses that are high traffic is Coffee News®. They place "good news" newsletters in businesses and sell ad space in the newsletters. As of 2012, they have 576 franchisees in the United States and

BUSINESS TIP

When you distribute these newsletters, make sure you do NOT personally deliver them. As a business owner, unless you are stopping by a top referral source or a client's office, that is a complete waste of time. You should have no problem finding someone who will run all over town for eight bucks an hour and a full tank of gas.

945 worldwide. Now personally, I think the advertising in these newsletters is awful. But the idea of getting into an environment where people are willing to sit down and read is excellent, and if done properly, it can work well for you too.

Idea No. 4 – Use Your Newsletter as Another Touch Mechanism Within a Direct Mail Campaign

BUSINESS TIP

My personal preference is to use the newsletter mailer as an additional step between steps two and three of your direct mail campaign. I have found this works the best. Of course, with any direct mail tip, the only way to know for sure is to test it out for yourself and track the results.

When you are mailing a direct mail campaign, time permitting, I have seen a huge increase in response when a newsletter is also mailed out separately to the prospect. Some people simply send their standard monthly newsletter, while others create a special newsletter that is a really well-disguised sales piece.

However you choose to do it, you can see a nice bump in your response rate by adding a newsletter step into the middle of a direct mail campaign. This is a strategy we use ourselves. Once you get in our funnel, we continue to send you a newsletter until we get some indication you aren't a good prospect anymore or are not interested. This has resulted in well over a million dollars in extra revenue for us over the years.

Idea No. 5 – Reactivate Former Customers

According to Bloomberg Business, 68 percent of consumers leave a business because they think the business doesn't care about them. Seriously! Think about that for a second—68 percent of people leave a company because they think the company doesn't care about them. If perception is reality, then at least 68 percent of the people who have ever done business with you think you don't care. That's crazy, right? Of course you care. These are the people paying you to keep your doors open and the lights on. These customers are the ones who allow you to pay your employees and feed your kids—literally. How can it be that they feel you don't care?

Have you ever heard the saying "actions speak louder than words"? Your customers feel this way because you don't show them you care. It's funny. Sometimes a company will try to show they care by sending an email thank-you card. Are you kidding me? In my mind, that is almost worse than doing nothing at all. It's kind of like saying, "We care, but not enough to spend any money on you, so we are just going to email you this card."

Consider this: Have you ever been on Facebook on your birthday and seen all those messages from people wishing you a happy birthday? Do those people really care about you? Of course they don't. Facebook told them it was your birthday, or they saw everyone else posting "Happy Birthday" and decided to join in on the fun. In the end, it's meaningless.

By sending your newsletter to people who have not bought your product or used your service recently and are now considered inactive, you can and will reactivate many of them. For the 68 percent who have left because they felt you didn't care, showing them that you do care will go a long way in winning them back.

I just heard a story from a caterer who sent his newsletter to clients who had not done business with him as far back as three years previously. After the first issue, those inactive clients produced $6,000 in new orders. Had he never sent the newsletter, those people would still be lost, and he would have

BUSINESS TIP

A reactivated previous customer is the third easiest type of person to sell to.

had almost NO chance of getting additional business or referrals from them. As he continues to mail his newsletter to these lost customers, he will see more and more of them coming back.

CHAPTER 11

Become a Good Pointer

A few years ago, I was awful at outsourcing and, even to some extent, at hiring employees to do tasks I could do myself. The reason I had this problem always seemed to come down to one of two issues.

1. I felt I could do "it" better than anyone else.

2. I was being cheap and didn't want to make an investment in my business.

What I found was that by trying to do everything myself and not investing in my business, my business plateaued. What I didn't realize at the time was that when you try to do

Building Relationships That Matter. Personal. Professional. Powerful.

everything yourself, inevitably you end up doing things that you're not good at, but you also end up doing many things you simply don't like and would prefer not to do. This causes all kinds of problems when trying to grow a business. I knew intellectually that I shouldn't be doing $8.00 an hour work. Also, intellectually, I knew that there were many people who could do the job better than I could, but for some reason, I couldn't let go.

Some of the reasons I struggled with letting go of tasks were partially due to a scarcity mindset I had at the time. A funny thing happened, though. I started to let go as I started to hire out tasks that I really wasn't good at and frankly didn't want to do. Almost immediately, I started to achieve more success in my business. Sales grew, profits went up, and I attracted more clients because the work I outsourced was being done better. Work even stopped feeling like work (most of the time, at least), and finally, I was happier than ever before. It is very important to focus on the few things in your business that you enjoy and that you are good at, and to let others do the rest for you. The same goes for your newsletter.

Below is a reprint of an article I wrote that details the system I use to get stuff off of my plate and to grow my business bigger, better, and faster.

* * *

Example Cover Article From "The Newsletter Pro" Monthly Print Newsletter:

Point Your Way to More Fun and Profits!

At the end of each year, I do two things religiously:

1. I work on my marketing calendar and my plan for my businesses for the upcoming year.

2. I reflect on areas where I didn't accomplish my goals for the previous year and try to pinpoint items I am currently doing in my business that quite simply, I don't find enjoyable.

Nearly every business owner knows they should have a business plan and a marketing calendar, so I don't want to focus on those activities in this article. What I want to look at is point No.2—reflecting on areas in my business and life where I did not achieve my goals, and the things that I'd prefer not to be doing in my business anymore. These two areas are more tied together than most people realize. In fact, I bet if you were to make a list (like I do) of things you weren't able to accomplish and the things you don't like doing, you will find that most of them are one in the same. If you don't like doing a certain type of project or task, you are far more likely to procrastinate in getting it done, which in turn means you don't complete all of your plans and goals for the year. It's a vicious cycle.

I have found that there is one surefire way to break this cycle of planning, procrastinating, and simply not getting your tasks done—become a better "pointer."

I believe I actually first heard the phrase "being a good pointer" from speaker and author Lee Milteer. Being a good pointer was described to me as being able to recognize the tasks and activities you are good at, as well as enjoy doing, and focus as much of your time as possible on those areas of your business. Now you take everything that is left (the stuff you don't want to do), and you simply "point," or instruct your employee, outsourcers, or other companies to do the "not so fun tasks" for you. Instantly you'll become happier and more productive because you are focusing on tasks you not only enjoy doing but you are likely good at to boot.

Building Relationships That Matter. Personal. Professional. Powerful.

Let me pull it all together with five easy steps you can take to implement this in your business right now.

Step 1 – Review any goals (written or otherwise) that have been around for so long now they are starting to feel like a pet.

Step 2 – Create a list of tasks that would need to be accomplished to get those goals completed and off your list.

Step 3 – Make a list of tasks you currently do in your business that you wish were no longer your responsibility.

Step 4 – Look at the lists from steps 2 and 3. Any tasks that are on both lists need to be assigned to another person/vendor. It is okay if you don't know who that is yet. If you see another task on the list from step 2 that someone else would be better suited to accomplish, go ahead and assign that as well.

Step 5 – Assign yourself the remaining tasks on the list from step 2 (these should mostly be tasks you enjoy and are good at).

Really that is all there is to it. I know it sounds simple. You may even think it sounds *too simple,* but just because it is simple doesn't mean it won't work.

If you'd like to know more or are ready to get started with your own custom newsletter, please give us a call at 208-297-5700 to schedule a no-pressure, completely free, consultation with a Pro. Or simply visit www.thenewsletterpro.com/schedule.

MY CHALLENGE TO YOU

The death of any good idea is time. Too often I meet people who told me six or 12 months ago that they wanted to get a newsletter started, but for one reason or another, they haven't done it. I know they understand the benefits, but they don't take action. And at the end of the day, nothing happens until someone takes action.

My challenge to you is to take action. You know how powerful newsletters are and how they can change your business, as newsletters have changed my business. When I started The Newsletter Pro in 2011, I knew newsletters were powerful, but I wouldn't have guessed they were this powerful. I underestimated how much relationships matter in business, as well as how long some people take to make a buying decision.

I recently calculated that a minimum of 29 percent of my "new" customers were receiving my newsletter for 13 months or more before they started using my service. Not building those relationships over time would have been very expensive in terms of lost revenue to my company. Don't lose out on nearly a third of your potential new business. Don't lose revenue from a customer attrition rate that is high but doesn't have to be. Use the tools and information in this book to solve those challenges. Following the formula laid out in this book will more than cover the costs associated with a newsletter.

If you are looking for help putting together a newsletter for your company, chat with a Pro on my team. To get on our calendar for a no-pitch, no-obligation call, go to www.thenewsletterpro.com/schedule or call 208-297-5700.

APPENDIX A

Business-to-Business Sample Articles

Business Management

Help Wanted: The Rules to Scoring Exceptional Employees

A good team is the foundation of any small business. In fact, the smaller the business, the more important it is to have a cohesive group that will rally together to get the job done. So from hiring to performance evaluations, and even in the case of those painful terminations, it's essential that you know what to look for when constructing a winning team.

You want to make sure that every member of your staff is willing to go above and beyond the call of duty. You want team members who adapt quickly when job descriptions or priorities shift—people who are willing to lend a helping hand even when it's not their job. These are the people who will do whatever it takes to get great results every time.

If you're busy trying to fit in, you'll never rise above the crowd. This maxim is as true in life as it is in the office. The ideal employee rises above because they are a little bit different from everyone else. They tend to be the spice of the office, adding flair and excitement to even the most mundane tasks. These individuals run the risk of pushing boundaries and challenging the status quo, but they also tend to come up with the most innovative ideas.

Speaking of acting out—the best team members know when to speak up and when to conform, as it benefits the group. It's important that everyone in the office can strike a balance between individuality and unity in order to succeed. Especially in stressful situations, collaboration is key.

Like any great friend, exceptional employees will help you celebrate the little things. They know when to publicly praise others and bring up the morale of the team as a whole. These are the people who highlight the successes of others and keep their criticisms private. They are also skilled in turning criticisms into opportunities for mutual growth.

That being said, these rare hires know when to speak up about a problem. Because of their inclusive and social nature, the ideal team member will have a good pulse on what others are thinking and be in tune with people's concerns. This is a perfect opportunity for them to speak on behalf of others and to raise important issues, so that everyone has their voice heard. Once these problems are vocalized, it becomes much easier to either address or resolve them and know that no resentment is stirring without the opportunity for resolution.

The final marker of an exceptional team member is someone who is extremely self-motivated. While others will complain that a task is impossible or too difficult, these go-getters don't consider failure an option. Somehow, no matter what comes their way, these people get the job done with time to spare. And when they have extra time, these are the people who constantly strive to improve.

Whether they are challenging outdated procedures, helping co-workers, tinkering with a new project, or taking on additional tasks, your best hires will always have something cooking on the back burner. The trick for you is to make sure that their natural drive is put to good use!

So how can you find these diamonds in the rough? The first step is to define what you believe to be the ideal person for the job. Discover which of these six traits resonate with the needs of your business and keep an eye out for people who meet the criteria.

Another tip is to always be on the lookout. Instead of interviewing applicants as jobs open up, you should be interviewing candidates continuously, building up a pool of potentially stellar hires. That way when you're in a moment of dire need, you'll have a few exceptional options to choose from.

Building Relationships That Matter. Personal. Professional. Powerful.

* * *

Business Did You Know

The Wisdom of Crowds: The Origin of True Intelligence

Here is a humbling thought: You are never smarter than the masses. No matter how high your IQ or what connections you have, your knowledge and abilities can never stand up to a crowd of average citizens, all working on the same question. Just ask the Good Judgment Project.

Over the last three years, the Good Judgment Project—the brainchild of three well-known psychologists and members of the CIA—has used the data of 3,000 average citizens to predict the political and sociological outcomes of events all over the world. And they are surprisingly accurate. Without any sort of professional or scholarly training, or any access to classified information, these individuals, who are of any age and have day jobs ranging from pharmacists to sanitation workers, make predictions that are used by the federal government.

How does it work? Participants in the experimental group go onto a website where they look at 12 carefully worded questions created by the intelligence community. The questions are time-relevant, asking individuals to predict the outcome of current global affairs. Beside each question is a place to write a number: the likelihood of that event occurring, according to the person sitting at the computer. Members don't have to justify their answers; they just have to put something down and see how right they turn out to be.

Within this group of 3,000 forecasters is a special group of "superforecasters"—individuals who are particularly good at making accurate predictions. How good is this team? Their predictions—once again made *without* access to classified information—are 30 percent more accurate than those of

CIA officers. But how can a group of people armed only with Google be more "intelligent" than a few well-trained, well-informed members of the CIA? It's called "the wisdom of crowds," and it's a concept that was discovered in 1906 by Francis Galton.

The story of Galton's discovery goes like this: Galton attended a fair where 800 people were trying to guess the weight of a dead ox (real entertainment in those days). After the event was over, Galton took the guesses home and noticed something interesting. While most of the guesses were either way too high or way too low, the average of the crowd's guesses was 1,198 pounds. The ox weighed 1,197 pounds. The radical numbers inevitably canceled each other out, while the truth remained at the center of the guesses. By averaging all those predictions together, an accurate answer was found.

So what does that mean for your business? People work better as a team. Whether you are a branch manager or a company CEO, when you work alone, you put limitations on your business. By "crowdsourcing" the members of your staff and allowing them to participate in a group discussion of where your company should go and what some potential methods would be for getting there, you have a better likelihood of succeeding. Things you might miss, others won't, and in that way, your company will be better informed, more efficient, and wiser.

Source: Spiegel, Alix. "So You Think You're Smarter Than a CIA Agent." NPR, 2 April 2014.

**

Employee Health

Why Encouraging Employees to Exercise is a Win-Win

We're heading toward a public health crisis where health care spending related to obesity is set to hit nearly $1 trillion by 2030. Of course, that's a tragic prediction, but how exactly does that relate to you and your business? Well, a business is only as productive as its employees are.

Interestingly, the Wellness Council of America found that "corporate fitness programs not only build camaraderie and morale, they can improve company bottom lines considerably. Improved worker health results in lower absenteeism, improved productivity, decreased health care costs, and fewer lawsuits." There's growing evidence to suggest that a small investment in worker fitness and health can actually be a big boost to a business's profitability!

How does that investment look? You could go big and subsidize a gym membership for everyone, buy some exercise equipment for the office, or simply offer time during the day for team members to go for a walk or jog. Another good idea is to start what's known as an "accountability program," where you encourage employees to set some fitness goals and turn the whole thing into a contest. Challenge employees to track the time they spend exercising or the number of steps they take every day. Finally, set aside time for the occasional meeting where the team can discuss their fitness progress and support each other.

Should you decide to host an accountability program, your business should consider sponsoring some prizes for the winner or winners. Some possible prizes could include an extra day of PTO, a gift certificate, or a nice dinner with the CEO.

Consider using a tool like www.dailyendorphin.com to track your fitness program, and even give away some inexpensive pedometers if you want to base the goal on number of steps. The point is, you can make fitness a fun group activity that helps everyone get to know each other better, while providing an enjoyable framework for improving the health of your team. Even morale is likely to go up when the team feels like you care about them as people, and want them happy and healthy. In the end, encouraging employee exercise is a win-win!

***

Mental Health

Not-So-Productive Habits: Secret Productivity Killers and How to Beat Them

Productivity: The way we combat the limited time in a day. We try to be as productive as possible, but the ordinary things we do every day hurt overall productivity. Here are a few common productivity killers and what you can do to break these bad habits.

Hitting the Snooze Button

"Just five more minutes" is appealing, but EOS Sleep's Dr. Matthew Mingrone warns against it. "Hitting the snooze button is, in fact, bad for sleep," he says. "[It] can leave you groggier and more tired than initially getting out of bed after the first alarm." Adrenaline and cortisol flood your body when it's jerked awake in the morning. Your stress response is triggered, and you feel alert. Letting yourself doze instead makes you disoriented and groggy.

How to Break the Habit

Set your alarm for later and go to sleep earlier. Program your alarm to go off when you actually need to get out of bed. If you're still feeling tired, try going to bed earlier. Even just half an hour can make a difference in feeling well-rested.

Multitasking

While it may create an illusion of progress, multitasking actually takes a bigger toll on your energy than your normal workload. By dividing your focus among a number of different tasks, each suffers from not having your full attention. The mental gear shift you go through when switching tasks drains mental energy. A study from Stanford University found that multitasking is less productive than simply focusing on a single task at a time.

How to Break the Habit

Give your complete attention to one task at a time. Make a to-do list of all the tasks that need to be accomplished. Allow yourself a certain amount of time for each task, and strive to finish in that time. Only when you're completely done with one task should you move on to another.

Eating Junk Food

When we feel overwhelmed during a busy day, it can be easy to justify snagging a donut for breakfast or chugging an energy drink for a pick-me-up. Not only is this unhealthy, it can also hamper your productivity. The brief energy spike we get from sugars fades fast. We soon need to refuel or else spend the rest of the day in a slump.

How to Break the Habit

Add healthier choices to your diet. *Entrepreneur* magazine suggests a "productivity diet" that includes eggs, yogurt, leafy greens, and salmon. A study published in the *British Journal of Health Psychology* found those who enjoyed fruits and vegetables during the day had more energy and addressed tasks with more creativity.

We'll never have more time in a day, but we can help ourselves use what time we do have better and more efficiently. Eliminating any one of these bad habits can result in an increase in productivity and overall wellness. Imagine what could happen if you got rid of all three!

APPENDIX B

Business-to-Consumer Sample Articles

Cover Article From "The Monthly Smile"

From Court to Field: We're Taking It Outside Once Again!

As the weather gets warmer, training is on my mind again. With a half marathon and bike relay on the radar for spring and summer, I've got my work cut out for me. Honestly, I wouldn't have it any other way! This is my favorite time of year, because with the changing of seasons comes more opportunities to get active outdoors and enjoy some fresh air with my exercise.

Just like this time last year, my family has started to make the annual shift from one sports season to another, taking the ball from the court to the field. For my daughters Allie and Brooklyn, that means going from a chaotic but strong basketball season to soccer practice. Our whole family loves everything basketball, so it's a little bittersweet when the season ends, but the girls have had such a fantastic time this year, with both Allie and Brooklyn playing on top teams. It has been a great experience for them both, and perhaps even more fun for their parents, who get to watch them learn and become stronger players.

Even though we're a family of runners and athletes, I often find myself very impressed with Nicole and her ability to perform so well in track. Her events are the 4x100 relay and the 100m hurdles. Running is something I genuinely enjoy and encourage, so I can fully understand the appeal of the relay, but the idea of jumping over things at the same time makes me nervous. Even talking to Nicole about jumping hurdles scares me! But she's got talent and drive, and she does a great job.

Brittany recently participated in Distinguished Young Women, a scholarship program in which the contestants are judged on their academic achievements, their interviewing skills, their talents and self-expression, and their fitness level. It was a great experience and opportunity for her and a fun evening out for us, and we're so proud of everything she's achieved in school and in her extracurricular.

I suppose even if our kids weren't doing great in school and on the court, we'd be proud, but Becca and I often say how lucky we are to have kids who put so much drive and enthusiasm into everything they do. As we prepare for longer days and more time outside, I hope you're making big plans to spend a little extra time with your family and friends, and to get some fresh air and exercise while you're at it!

– Dr. Brown

* * *

Human Interest Article

Uphill Both Ways . . . in Scrubs?

The winter madness in the South this past January quickly reached legendary proportions, and with all of the pileups, slide offs, and jam-packed roadways, a few heroes slipped through. Meet Dr. Zenko Hrynkiw. He's just your average Alabama neurosurgeon, and nobody goes unattended on his watch. Amid the erratic weather and insane road conditions, Dr. Hrynkiw was doing his usual work—saving lives—when a call came in.

The good doctor was told that at another hospital across town, a patient was dying. As he tells it, this patient was looking at a "90 percent chance of death," and there was nobody at the facility who could take on the surgery. Normally, the six-mile drive would have taken just minutes, but with the weather-induced madness on the roadways, an ambulance wasn't going to get anywhere very quickly. So Dr. Hrynkiw went about his business as any logical man of science and community would do: In his scrubs and a heavy coat, he set out on foot (he was even still wearing his operating room slip-ons).

As he took to the streets, he tumbled down a hill, helped to push out a few vehicles that had taken a turn on the ice, and stopped to defrost at an ambulance that wasn't moving. Finally, he got a lift on his last leg of the journey and reached the hospital, rushed into surgery, and saved his patient's life. Let's all take a moment and appreciate that, aside from being awesome, Dr. Hrynkiw is also 62 years old and thinks nothing of his heroics! "I walk a lot," he says, "so it wasn't a big deal." The doc then stayed at the hospital for the remainder of the week, because "there was too much work to be done."

***

General Interest/Mental Health

Stop One-Daying Yourself to Death

Many people think about success as a future event. They say, "One day I'm going to be a millionaire," or "One day I'm going to be an inspirational speaker," or "One day I'm going to be famous."

We all do it. We all have our "one day" goals or aspirations, but this "one day" mentality projects our success sometime into the far-flung future. A large problem with living in the future is that you're not experiencing a vibrant and fulfilling life right now. You're not noticing the richness and knowledge that others have to offer you, nor the opportunities that continually crop up around you. If you want to achieve success, your "one day" needs to begin today.

How do you know you're living in the present? There are a few signals.

1. **You feel revved up and ready to go.** If you're no longer projecting your success into the future, but rather on the "today," then your energy and your focus is acute and centered.

2. **You don't experience fear or guilt.** If you're not focusing on the past, you can eliminate guilt, and if you're not thinking about the future, then you can eliminate fear. There is no room for fear and guilt in success!

3. **You're calm and focused.** If you're not fretting over past mistakes or fearing possible future challenges, then you can focus entirely on the tasks at hand.

4. **You're making headway in future goals.** Living in the moment means that you're ultimately planning for the future. Your actions have long-lasting effects on what happens in your future.

Your choices take on a new sense of importance when you're living in the present. Everything matters right now.

Living in the moment, focusing your energy on what is taking place today, and enjoying your present opportunities is empowering. It means living consciously and knowing how your thoughts and actions affect your life. So regardless of what your "one day" goal is, make sure you're putting the steps into motion today to make it a reality.

Building Relationships That Matter. Personal. Professional. Powerful.

***

Family Article

How to Make the Dog Days More Bearable: Create a Summer Bucket List

Do you remember the dog days of summer? Anyone who grew up before the fateful invention of the internet knows that a three-month summer break felt like an eternity by mid-July. If you weren't playing sports or doing chores, chances are you were facing down that tidal wave of boredom, and those "I'm bored" moments were a nightmare for parents.

As a grown-up, your relationship with boredom is different. With a busy schedule, you likely relish having no plan, no place to go, and no one to see. For kids, modern entertainment and technology keeps them more stimulated than ever before, but that doesn't mean they're happy. In fact, *Psychology Today* reports too much screen time disrupts sleep and desensitizes the brain's reward system, causing kids to be more irritable, exhausted, and depressed. In other words, computers aren't great babysitters.

The truth is, there is *always* something for the kiddos to do. It's simply a matter of peeling their fingers away from their iPads and teaching them what summer is all about. Sit the family down and create a summer bucket list. Grab a big piece of paper or a whiteboard and start jotting down activities. Let the kids help create the list. They'll probably come up with some less-attainable ideas (financially or logistically), but it's good for them dream! If you can't cross it off the list this summer, maybe it's a big goal to work on for next summer. That said, encourage free or inexpensive activities. With better weather, outdoor activities in the park or backyard are easier. Add gardening, water-balloon fights, stargazing, and chalk art to the list. These activities are so classically enjoyable, even the gloomiest adult can have fun.

Keep adding to the list until you run out of ideas. Once the summer bucket list has been made, tack it to the wall and refer to it when you need an idea to cure the boredom. This exercise alone teaches kids to use their imagination and helps them better understand the value of time. As an added bonus, if your kids aren't easily motivated to do chores or yard work, the bigger ticket items on the list might serve as rewards for good behavior and hard work. After all, summer wouldn't be summer without a little sweat—just like the good old days.

Building Relationships That Matter. Personal. Professional. Powerful.

NEED HELP WITH YOUR NEWSLETTER? TALK TO THE PROS.

Schedule a complimentary consultation with our team by visiting www.thenewsletterpro.com/schedule.

Made in the USA
San Bernardino, CA
12 July 2017